# ghosts

Praise for *Ghosts: A Haunted History*

'Lisa Morton's brisk, handsomely illustrated *Ghosts: A Haunted History* canters through millennia of supposed uncanny interruptions with a kind of puckish scepticism . . . Morton excels at presenting us with instances of the persistence of belief, across all times and cultures . . . there are moments all the same when the hint of something truly uncanny is permitted to intrude.' – *TLS*

'*Ghosts* is intelligent and well structured. It's also well informed, which is apparent in the sheer volume of spectral examples that Morton has collected . . . the perfect companion for those who err towards skepticism over embellishment, yet still find themselves riddled in goose-pimples when they hear a creak in the floorboards in the dead of night.' – *Rue Morgue* magazine

'In *Ghosts*, Lisa Morton brings her encyclopedic knowledge of folklore and the supernatural to bear on this vast, vital subject. For students of "things that go bump in the night" the book is simply indispensable.' – Leslie S. Klinger, author of *The New Annotated H. P. Lovecraft*

'*Ghosts* is brilliant, insightful and scary as hell. Lisa Morton proves that truth is definitely stranger than fiction.'
– Jonathan Maberry, *New York Times* bestselling author of *The Nightsiders* and *Ghostwalkers*

LISA MORTON

# ghosts

## A HAUNTED HISTORY

REAKTION BOOKS

Published by
Reaktion Books Ltd
Unit 32, Waterside
44–48 Wharf Road
London N1 7UX, UK
www.reaktionbooks.co.uk

First published 2015
First paperback edition 2017, reprinted 2022
Copyright © Lisa Morton 2015

Printed and bound in Great Britain
by Clays Ltd, Elcograf S.p.A.

A catalogue record for this book is available from the British Library

ISBN 978 1 78023 843 2

# Contents

Halloween ghost decoration, Studio City, California, 2012.

# Introduction

*On a gloomy autumn day, as dead leaves scud around your feet
and a chill breeze finds its way under your collar, you approach
the house in which you grew up. It's a month since your father
was laid to rest in the family plot beside your mother. You've
dealt with relatives and the funeral and the initial bills, you've
mourned and have come to accept that he's gone, and now you
have to settle his estate.*

*You moved out of this house twenty years ago, and even
though you've visited many times since, it feels strange now,
almost alien. You see, as if for the first time, how run-down
it is – the white paint is peeling, the old oak tree in the front
garden is dying, the fence is in bad need of repair.*

*It isn't until you enter the house, however, that the melan-
choly really hits you. The house smells of sickness – the long,
damnable disease that finally took your father – and it's cold,
since the heating hasn't been on for a month. There are shadows
everywhere, and even though you know everything in this
house (there's the shelf of books you read a dozen times, here's
the table they said your great-grandfather made), you've never
been alone here as an adult, and an inexplicable shiver races
through you.*

*The stairs creak as you climb them. A pipe groans as a stray
breeze passes through it. Your old room still has posters from
your adolescence, and this at least offers some comfort. You fall
back on the bed, close your eyes . . .*

*And awaken to the sure knowledge that someone is in the room.*

*It's dark now, nearly full night, and the room is chilled. Over by the window, limned by the faint glow of streetlights, is a figure. You hold your breath, paralysed by fear; you can't move, can't even cry out. The dim apparition turns to you, your heart hammers . . . and suddenly you're alone. The room warms again, and it takes you a few seconds to realize the lingering scent in the air is your father's aftershave.*

You've just met something you can describe only as a ghost. Your experience is so common throughout all times and regions of human history that it's close to being universal . . . and yet no solid proof has ever been offered to prove the existence of life after death. Nearly half of all Americans currently believe in ghosts (and more than a third believe they have lived in a haunted house), and in other countries belief runs even higher (for example, 87 per cent of Taiwan's office workers believe in them).[1] Ghosts are found in everything from classic literature to contemporary reality television shows, and yet even defining ghosts is surprisingly difficult and a source of debate among aficionados. The English ghost-hunter Peter Underwood described ten types of ghost, including haunted objects, 'elementals' (ghosts connected to particular locations – these often provoke severe reactions, such as insanity, in onlookers) and ghosts of the living (see, for example, the Scottish belief in the 'fetch', an apparition of a living individual that might appear to a loved one as an omen or warning).

The ghost, in the classic sense, is thought to be the spirit of someone who has died. Encounters with ghosts are – as in the scenario that opened this introduction – often connected to architecture and family ties, especially those that are wrapped up in grief, and may include 'cold spots' (an area of a house or room where the temperature is inexplicably lower), rapping or banging sounds, music, smells and the sensation of being touched.

As humanity has spread and changed, so have its ghost beliefs. Improvements in science and technology have allowed us

<table>
<tr><td colspan="4" align="center"><u>**Seller Disclosures**</u><br>Check YES or NO to the answers to the questions below.</td></tr>
<tr><td>1. Are you aware of Mello-Roos tax, Landscape Maintenance Districts, School Bonds, or other fees and/or assessments attached to, or associated with, the Subject Property?</td><td>☐ YES</td><td>☐ NO</td><td>If YES, see item 5 below</td></tr>
<tr><td>2. Are you aware of any settlement received or judgments regarding a lawsuit involving you the Seller, the Subject Property, tract/development, or the Homeowners Association?<br>If Yes:</td><td>☐ YES</td><td>☐ NO</td><td>If YES, see item 5 below</td></tr>
<tr><td>a) Were repairs or other remedial actions made to the Subject Property?</td><td>☐ YES   ☐ NO</td><td>☐ UNKNOWN</td><td>If YES, see item 5 below</td></tr>
<tr><td>b) Were the repairs or remedial actions done with appropriate permits?</td><td>☐ YES   ☐ NO</td><td>☐ UNKNOWN</td><td>If NO, see item 5 below</td></tr>
<tr><td>3. Has anything "stigmatized" the Subject Property such as a death on the property, a violent crime, crime in the area/neighborhood, or allegations that the Subject Property is "haunted"?</td><td>☐ YES</td><td>☐ NO</td><td>If YES, see item 5 below</td></tr>
</table>

'Haunted' clause from a standard American
real estate disclosure agreement, 2014.

to investigate the nature of ghosts; while some investigators have sought to use new devices to capture proof of the existence of the frustratingly elusive undead, others have experimented with the human brain in an effort to find non-supernatural explanations for ghosts. Mental illness, repressed trauma, the hypnagogic state experienced between sleep and wakefulness, electromagnetic fields and extreme low-frequency infrasound have all been advanced as theories to explain the experience of encountering a ghost, although a single explanation has yet to be widely accepted – or at least as widely accepted as the notion that a ghost is a spirit of the dead.

If ghosts are, in fact, no more than hallucinations, perhaps brought about by exposure to insufficient electrical shielding or certain inaudible low-frequency sound waves, then the question remains: why do these visions so often take the form of a foggy human shape, one that occasionally coalesces and assumes the features of someone we know, usually a deceased loved one? And why are these encounters almost always so terrifying? Wouldn't meeting a dead spouse or sibling be wondrous, even joyous in revealing the existence of an afterlife? In her nineteenth-century classic *The Night-side of Nature*, the writer Catherine Crowe suggests that the fear of ghosts arises simply from 'bad training', while the Spiritualism movement that her book influenced also sought out ghosts as a source of enlightenment. Yet, by the end of that century, fiction writers such as Charles Dickens, F. Marion Crawford and M. R. James had returned the ghost to the realm of the frightening.

Surely it is no coincidence that throughout humankind's written history, ghost stories have been prevalent in religion, mythology and literature. Our earliest recorded epics – *Gilgamesh*, *The Odyssey* – all combine heroic journeys with frightening visits from ghosts. Ghost stories have often been associated with war – which is, after all, an activity that often leads to death – and soldiers make for unassailably stalwart and honest protagonists in ghost stories (as do lawyers, doctors and ministers of the church).

Ghosts have been institutionalized and turned into festivals – China's *Hungry Ghost Festival*, or Mexico's *Dias de los Muertos* – and by the eighteenth century the ghost story was an established genre of Western literature. Gothic writers like Ann Radcliffe (whose hauntings were all revealed as hoaxes by the end of each of her novels) and Horace Walpole popularized ghost stories even more, and paved the way for later writers such as Dickens (*A Christmas Carol* may be the most famous ghost story of all time) and Bram Stoker, who applied many of the techniques of the classic ghost story to eastern European vampire folklore, creating *Dracula* in the process.

By the end of the nineteenth century, Spiritualism was in vogue. Well-to-do Victorians and Edwardians throughout both Britain and America swarmed into mediums' parlours, hoping a séance would lead to a message from Uncle Henry or a glimpse of ghostly ectoplasm. The latter was believed to be an emanation from the beyond, but was instead revealed to be a few yards of chiffon hidden away by the medium before the start of the proceedings.

Even though the psychics of the Spiritualism craze and the accompanying interest in 'spirit photography' were all debunked by the likes of magicians J. N. Maskelyne and Harry Houdini, and the fad had largely faded by the 1930s, belief in ghosts had not. The growing popularity of horror literature – which exploded in the 1970s as the work of Stephen King hit bookshops and cinema screens generated screams with films like *The Exorcist* and *The Omen* – led to a resurgence of interest in classic ghost tales, and the arrival of reality television brought with it a veritable haunted house-full of ghost-hunting and paranormal investigation programmes.

So, nearly 5,000 years after the first recorded ghost stories, we are still encountering spirits from beyond and scaring one another with fictionalized accounts. Our thirst to believe has not changed, even if our means of transmission have.

Oh, and we're still not sure.

Before we begin our own ghost adventure, however, it's necessary to define exactly what we're looking for. Surprisingly, that's not as easy as you might think.

# I
# What Are (and Are Not) Ghosts?

When we hear the word 'ghost', most of us immediately think of something barely glimpsed or translucent, the spirit of someone who has died. If we give it a few more seconds of consideration, we might imagine a fearful event in a dark, isolated place, or perhaps even a frightening story we have read or a film we have seen.

However, despite certain culturally shared notions, defining a 'ghost' is not a simple undertaking. In our contemporary, Western thinking, the ghost is the spirit of a deceased individual that manifests itself to us after their death; but in the past, and in other cultures, the ghost may be very different. Belief in ghosts seems to be nearly universal, but the shape the undead spirit takes varies according to the particular society's collective imagination.

Even in our own Western European tradition, the very word 'ghost' has altered in both meaning and form over the last five or so centuries. According to the *Oxford English Dictionary*, the word was originally derived from the German word *gást*, which in turn evolved out of the pre-Teutonic *gaisto-z* or *ghoizdo-z*, meaning 'fury, anger'; until about 1590 'ghost' referred to the essence of life, rather than the survival after death. This original meaning survives in the phrase 'give up the ghost', which dates back to at least 1388, when a translation of Matthew 27: 50 stated: 'Jhesus eftsoone criede with a greet voyce and gaf vp the goost.' This use of the word also survives in the name 'Holy Ghost', the third part of the Christian Trinity. The Holy Ghost probably has its roots in the Hebrew *ruah ha-qodesh*; *ruah* originally meant 'breath' or 'wind', and *ruah ha-qodesh* was the holy breath of God that inspired human beings.[1] The fourth-century Latin translation of the Bible rendered this as *spiritus sanctus*, with *spiritus* again referring to 'breath' or 'wind', and by the time of Middle English, the phrase had become *holi gost*.

The use of 'ghost' to refer to a dead spirit that appears to the living first became popular about the time of Geoffrey Chaucer, who in 'Dido, Queen of Carthage' (part III of *The Legend of Good Women, c.* 1385) refers to 'This night my fadres gost hath in my sleep so sore me tormented.' When Shakespeare wrote *Hamlet* (some time between 1599 and 1602), the modern meaning was sufficiently established for a ghost to be included as a major character in the play, complete with the vengeful purpose now frequently ascribed to ghosts. In his poem 'Venus and Adonis', Shakespeare also imbues ghosts with the modern qualities of fear and omens:

> Look, how the world's poor people are amazed
> At apparitions, signs and prodigies,
> Whereon with fearful eyes they long have gazed,
> Infusing them with dreadful prophecies.

In this same poem, Death is described as a 'grim-grinning ghost', a phrase that would later become the title of the theme music to Disneyland's famous ghost ride, the Haunted Mansion.

Shakespeare also provides the word as a verb, when, in *Antony and Cleopatra* (II.6), Pompey refers to Julius Caesar 'who at Philippi he good Brutus ghosted'. In the military, the use of 'ghost' as a verb is applied to a soldier who avoids duty, and in modern British slang, to 'ghost' is to move prisoners at night.[2]

The word has also been twisted into new nouns, manifesting as 'ghostess' and 'ghostlet', to describe (respectively) a female ghost and a small ghost. Other uses of the word have referred simply to a corpse, to a photograph, to something that lacks force (as in 'he doesn't stand the ghost of a chance') or to someone who secretly performs the work of another (a 'ghostwriter'). In addition, the word has lent itself to wry slang usage. In the theatre world, for instance, 'the ghost walks' means that salary will finally be forthcoming to

Hamlet sees his father's ghost on the battlements.
Illustration by Robert Dudley, published as a chromolithograph, 1856–8.

cast and crew. 'Ghost turds' are 'accumulations of lint found under furniture'.[3]

What about the concept behind the word? If a ghost is the spirit of a dead person, how does that differ from a soul? 'Soul' is today synonymous with the original meaning of 'ghost' – the essential life force of a human being. Whereas 'ghost' has come to refer to that essence after death, most religions believe that a soul is possessed by all living persons, and that the soul survives in some form after death. Where 'soul' and 'ghost' deviate most, however, is in the interaction with the living: a ghost must be seen, heard or otherwise experienced in a tangible way by the living.

When seen, ghosts are typically described as translucent or dim; they cannot be grasped, although a mortal unlucky enough to encounter one may experience being touched, feeling suddenly cold or smelling a particular scent that meant something to the ghost when alive. A ghostly visitor who was subjected to a gruesome ending may or may not show signs of that bloody demise. The form of the ghost may even shift as it is viewed; in ancient cultures, some spirits suddenly took on animal forms. Occasionally the ghost may appear so solid that it is initially indistinguishable from a human being.

Ghosts need not be confined to the spirits of deceased persons, however: ghost animals are also prevalent in many cultures. In Britain, for example, ghostly hounds are common and accompany a spectral huntsman sometimes named Gabriel Ratchets or Herne the Hunter. Although some who encountered this terrifying pack believed them to be diabolical in nature, rather than ghostly, there were other notions surrounding them, as well: 'In the neighbour-hood of Leeds these hounds are known as "Gabble Ratchets", and are supposed, as in other places, to be the souls of unbaptized children who flit restlessly about their parents' abode.'[4] In Cornwall, an old folk belief held that any girl who died after being heart-broken by a deceitful man would return as a white hare to haunt her beloved. This white hare would invariably cause the man's death.

The world's religions treat ghosts in a variety of ways. Judaism and Christianity take a dim view, as outlined in the story of Saul and the Witch (or Medium) of Endor. After the death of the leader and prophet Samuel, Saul (the king of Israel) bans all mediums. How-ever, when the army of the Philistines assembles against him and he receives no direction from God, Saul disguises himself and seeks

George Cruikshank, *Herne the Huntsman*, 19th-century engraving.

out the Witch of Endor. She recognizes him and initially suspects a trap, but Saul swears that he only seeks advice from the spirit of Samuel, and assures her safety. She brings forth the spirit, who admonishes Saul for going against the word of God, and warns him of a great defeat in the battle against the Philistines.

Ghosts often imparted equally dour news in older religions, as well. In Book XI of Homer's *Odyssey*, Ulysses sacrifices sheep to gain access to the ghost of Tiresias, a great prophet. The 'shades' arrive making terrible screaming sounds, drink the blood of the sheep, talk about the darkness of the underworld and foretell great misfortune for the rest of Ulysses' journey. And in the Sumerian tale 'Gilgamesh, Enkidu and the Nether World' (dating from about 2000 BCE), the ghost of Gilgamesh's friend Enkidu returns to warn the great hero that any description of the afterlife would make him 'sit down and weep'.[5]

Where do ghosts and deities intersect? In the first volume of his *Principles of Sociology*, the famed nineteenth-century philosopher and polymath Herbert Spencer suggested that 'deities are the expanded ghosts of dead men.'[6] Ghosts may also be synonymous with demons, as in the western Indian belief in the *bhūta*, a demon that is the spirit of someone who was malicious in life, which may cause harm in death by possessing the living, creating storms or causing disease.

Is a dead spirit encountered in a dream a ghost? Seeing a dead loved one in a dream dates as far back as Homer's *Iliad*, in which the hero, Achilles, is visited in his sleep by his beloved friend Patroclus, who pleads for a proper burial and for vengeance. In contemporary culture, psychologists refer to these as 'visitation dreams', and suggest that 'the dreams we have while grieving are an important part of that process.'[7] Similarly, what of spirits who might be glimpsed while the viewer is in an extreme mental state, such as religious ecstasy? During the Middle Ages, Christian mystics often wrote of speaking with the dead while experiencing ecstatic states. The thirteenth-century nun Gertrude of Helfta, for example, described meeting deceased sisters of the cloth, lay brothers and even a knight during her extensive and excruciating

After Henry Fuseli, *Achilles Grasping for the Shade of Patroclus*, 1806, engraving.

physical suffering (which was caused by various diseases). The apparitions encountered in dreams and visions operate much like their more earthbound cousins in some respects, by delivering warnings or prophecies, but differ greatly in others: they seldom arouse fear, and they are experienced by only one person, usually only a single time. Given that these spirits serve a more obvious psychological function and cannot be encountered by more than one individual, for the purposes of this book they will be considered as outside the realm of true ghosts.

If a ghost is essentially a soul that returns to mortal existence and is experienced in some fully wakeful way by the living, is a ghost different from a phantom, an apparition, a spirit or a spectre? In fact, these words are all essentially synonyms for 'ghost'. 'Wraith', however, is one of the more curious alternative words; although it is often used interchangeably with 'ghost', a wraith is technically the spirit of someone who is still alive. In Scottish folklore, a wraith (or 'fetch') may appear to warn a loved one or friend; at other times, the wraith is seen at the very moment of its owner's death. In one of the best-known fetch tales, the Earl of Cornwall has a strange encounter with his good friend William Rufus while hunting in a forest:

> He advanced beyond the shades of the woods on to the moors above them, and he was surprised to see a very large black goat advancing over the plain. As it approached him, which it did rapidly, he saw that it bore on its back 'King Rufus', all black and naked, and wounded through in the midst of his breast. Robert adjured the goat, in the name of the Holy Trinity, to tell what it was he carried so strangely. He answered, 'I am carrying your king to judgment; yea, that tyrant William Rufus, for I am an evil spirit, and the revenger of that malice which he bore to the Church of God . . .'. Having so spoken, the spectre vanished. Robert, the earl, related the circumstance to his followers, and they shortly after learned that at that very hour William Rufus had been slain.[8]

Although the word 'revenant' is sometimes used for 'ghost', revenant more accurately refers to a dead person who returns in a physical body. A revenant is usually tied to violence – a victim who reanimates to continue a cycle of murder and terror. In his tale *The Devil's Elixir* (1815), E.T.A. Hoffmann assigns the revenant the character of the supernaturally lost: 'I was like a condemned spirit – like a *revenant*, doomed involuntarily to wander on the earth.'[9] When the revenant returned in corporeal form to feed on the blood of the living, it was a vampire.

Ghosts also have curious ties to other supernatural entities. The Babylonian *edimmu* is usually thought to be a ghost, but it also appears in lists of demons that afflict human beings. The second-century CE writer Apuleius, in *The God of Socrates*, refers to ghosts as demons, and even goes so far as to suggest that good souls can produce good demons. The early Christian writer Tertullian wrote in about 200 CE of 'the deceit perpetrated by evil spirits that conceal themselves in the characters of the dead'.[10] And in Chinese, the word *gui* refers to both dead and divine spirits. While ghosts are clearly separated from such creatures as vampires – because the latter continue in physical form after death – in some mythologies it is less clear where ghosts end and demons or gods begin.

The European monster known as the *gello* aptly demonstrates the confusion that sometimes surrounds the ghostly and the demonic. First appearing in a poetry fragment by Sappho, the *gello* was a creature that was thought to murder infants and small children by sucking their blood. A human being might become a *gello* after death, gaining demonic qualities even while retaining human distinctions such as gender (demons are believed to be sexless). The debate over the nature of the *gello* ignited controversy among eighth-century Christian theologians, who extended belief in the creature to belief in the spiritual nature of Jesus. Even though the Church's official position was to deny the existence of the *gello*, infant-murdering spirits called *gelloudes* are still thought to terrorize areas of rural Greece.

Whether divine, demonic or merely ghostly, these spirits often return to deliver menacing portents to the living. But the ghost is not always a messenger of doom. Both the Chinese and the Latin Americans celebrate festivals (*Yu Lan*, or the Hungry Ghost Festival, and *Dias de los Muertos*, or Days of the Dead, respectively) in which they believe that the ghosts of their deceased relatives return to their families and must be offered the food and drink they enjoyed while alive. In both situations the spirits are essentially harmless, although a high price may be paid by the living who fail to propitiate their ancestors in a suitable manner.

In European culture, on the other hand, the ghost retained a frightening, ominous reputation throughout the classical world and into the Middle Ages. In ancient Greece and Rome, an encounter with a ghost usually meant certain death (unless it was the ghost of a hero); ghosts were sometimes employed by sorcerers and witches to bring about the death of an unwitting victim. By the time of the Enlightenment, ghosts were often associated with ruins and old structures. The late eighteenth- and early nineteenth-century practitioners of Gothic literature – Horace Walpole, Ann Radcliffe, Matthew Lewis – used ghosts to generate fear in their fiction. As the character Bianca notes in Walpole's classic *The Castle of Otranto* (1764), 'Oh! dear Lady, I would not speak to a ghost for the world!'[11]

The meaning of ghosts shifted again in the late nineteenth century, with the arrival of the Spiritualism craze in Europe and America. The ghost was no longer a creature to be feared, a wispy, chill-inducing shade associated with the gloomy remains of ruined abbeys and mansions; rather, the ghost of a deceased loved one could be reliably and safely produced by a medium (for a fee, of course) and required to answer simple questions.

The nineteenth century brought another fresh take on ghosts, however: for the first time scepticism – in response to Spiritualism – was widespread and well-argued. In his book *The Supernatural?* (1891), Lionel A. Weatherly proposes a system of classification for apparitions that is very different from Peter Underwood's ten types of ghost. Weatherly suggests that ghosts are the result of: 1. common deception and trickery; 2. mistaken identity; 3. illusion; and 4. hallucination.[12]

Even though the mediums of Spiritualism were swiftly discredited, the new ghost was an entity that could be measured and questioned. As technology and psychology changed throughout the twentieth century, so did the ghost; on one hand, Sigmund Freud associated fear of ghosts with a 'castration-complex' and suggested: 'Most likely our fear still contains the old belief that the deceased becomes the enemy of his survivor and wants to carry him off to share his new life with him.'[13] On the other hand, scientific advances sought to provide proof of the existence of the ghost ... and were unsuccessful. Yet a quick glance at twenty-first-century horror films and books will demonstrate that the ghost retains tremendous power to terrify otherwise rational, sophisticated adults.

# 2

# Lands of the Dead:
# Early Sightings

Looking back to the earliest records made by human beings –
primitive cave paintings found throughout Europe, dating back
to the Paleolithic age – it is tempting to view images of giant animals
and imagine them as the ghosts of the prey our ancestors hunted.
Indeed, it's not hard to imagine the earliest hunter-gatherers of Africa
or the cave-dwellers of Lascaux gathering around a campfire at the
end of a day to share tales of exciting battles with other mammals,
even as they cast nervous glances back, wondering how many of
their dead kin were waiting just beyond the reach of the flames' glow.

But the truth is that we have no way of knowing what our pre-
historic forebears thought about the afterlife; the absence of written
records leaves the cave art open to interpretation and guesswork.
There is evidence that early man had specific funeral practices –
corpses were often buried with a few items and with their legs drawn
up – which does suggest that they prepared their dead for some
sort of afterlife.

The first written histories all refer to ghosts in some form. In
the texts of ancient Mesopotamia (dating back to about 2,500 BCE),
in addition to the tale of the ghost of Gilgamesh's friend Enkidu
(referred to in chapter One), belief in ghosts called *edimmu* was
also widespread: 'The êdimmu . . . is generally, but wrongly, read
êkimmu, and translated "the seizer", from êkemu, "to seize". In reality,
however, it was an ordinary spirit, and the word is used for the wraiths
of the departed.'[1] Edimmu could possess people or cause illness; an
elaborate exorcism ritual called for wrapping white and black yarn

about the victim and calling on the god Merodach. In one Babylonian account of the Creation, *edimmu* is the flesh of a god, and is released to become a ghost upon death (animals do not possess *edimmu*). If the newly deceased receive a proper burial and respectful offerings, the *edimmu* will be benevolent, but if the burial or offerings are lacking, the ghost will be angry and, seeking vengeance, will inflict disease on its living kin.

In Chinese culture, the ghost often functions in a way similar to the Western (Catholic) notion of souls trapped in Purgatory: ghosts are souls that are stuck in the transition from Earth to Heaven, although they may also be trapped in Hell. In the traditional Buddhist legend 'Moginlin Saving his Mother from Hades', a man finds out that his mother's ghost is in Hell, where she is being tortured with starvation. Moginlin sets off on a treacherous journey through the underworld, but when he reaches his mother's ghost and offers her food, the food burns up before she can consume it. The Buddha offers Moginlin a chance to save his mother by finding ten monks to pray for her on the fifteenth day of the seventh lunar month, and her ghost is finally released from its suffering to move on. This story is a mainstay of the Buddhist festival known as Ullambana, which has been incorporated into the modern celebration of the Hungry Ghost Festival, celebrated – as per the legend – on the fifteenth day of the seventh month.

In horror films, ancient Egypt is frequently home to shambling, murderous mummies, but in reality the mummies are part of dynastic Egypt's complex mythology and embody an extraordinary set of ghost beliefs. The Egyptians believed in not simply a single soul, but multiple soul-like essences that combined to form an individual. The *ka* was a spirit placed into an infant at birth, and forcibly separated from it at death; it always lingered close to the body, and so was typically thought to inhabit the tomb, where it was provided with the food, drink and other necessities that it had enjoyed in its physical form during life. The *ba* was the personality that defined each person, and the *akh* undertook the perilous voyage into the afterlife, where – if it survived a series of tests and trials – it would eventually stand before Osiris to be judged. The preservation of the body, or mummification (a skill that reached its peak during the Twenty-first Dynasty, about 1000 BCE), was a necessary part of allowing the *akh* to seek eternal life. Also assisting the *akh* was a large set of nearly 1,200 spells to help it confront the perils of the afterlife; these 'Coffin Texts' were later gathered into *The Book of the Dead*, and were usually painted on the interior of sarcophagi or coffins.

Ghosts were an accepted part of the ancient Egyptian world, and paying proper respect to the ancestral dead was one way to ensure success and avoid harm. Accidents and tragedies might be ascribed to ghosts; an animal attack, for instance, might have been instigated by a dead spirit. Letters were written to the ghosts of deceased loved ones seeking aid in family disputes; only a handful of such letters have survived, but historians suggest that it is likely that the Egyptians also addressed their dead kin orally.

The ghosts of ancient Egypt were sometimes thought to be especially drawn to children, who might find their breath sucked away by the spectre's decayed, mummified lips, or might simply be frightened to death by the fearsome thing. Mothers often made a charm of lettuce, garlic, tow (straw), bones and honey, and sang a lullaby to their little ones at night, rendered in rather quaint translation in the early twentieth century:

> Oh, avaunt! Ye ghosts of night,
> Nor do my baby harm;
> Ye may come with steps so light,
> But I'll thwart you with my charm.
>
> For my babe you must not kiss,
> Nor rock if she should cry –
> Oh! if you did aught amiss,
> My own, my dear, would die.
>
> O ye dead men, come not near –
> Now I have made the charm –
> There's lettuce to prick you here,
> Garlic with smell to harm;

There's tow to bind like a spell,
The magic bones are spread;
There's honey the living love well –
'Tis poison to the dead.[2]

Ghosts appear frequently in the surviving texts of the ancient Greeks, and the historian Daniel Ogden identifies four specific types: *aôroi*, 'those dead before their time' (mainly children); *bi(ai)-othanatoi*, 'those dead by violence'; *agamoi*, 'those dead before marriage'; and *ataphoi*: 'those deprived of burial'.[3] Although the Greek and Roman ghosts have much in common with their later kin – they are, for example, prone to appear in dreams, and often seek vengeance – they are more commonly found in graveyards than in houses. Both the philosopher Socrates and the fourth-century emperor Constantius II mention ghosts being near tombs, and the latter even created a law in 357 CE that put to death sorcerers who robbed graves and 'collected' ghosts.

The Roman writer Apuleius, in *The God of Socrates*, created a Latin list of ghosts:

There is also another species of demons, according to a second signification, and this is the human soul, after it has performed its duties in the present life, and quitted the body: I find that this is called in the ancient Latin language by the name of Lemur. Now, of these Lemures, the one who, undertaking the guardianship of his posterity, dwells in a house with propitious and tranquil influence, is called the 'familiar' Lar. But those who, having no fixed habitation of their own, are punished with vague wandering, as with a kind of exile, on account of the evil deeds of their life, are usually called 'Larvæ', thus becoming a vain terror to the good, but a source of punishment to the bad. But when it is uncertain what is the allotted condition of any one of these, and whether it is Lar or Larva, it is called a God Manes; the name of God being added for the sake of honour.[4]

However, other Roman scholars suggested that only the *manes* were good spirits, while both the *lemures* and the *larvæ* were violent (the *larvæ* are sometimes compared to the modern classification of 'elementals', aggressive ghosts that are often linked with a particular area). The Roman festival Lemuria, which took place in May, involved the following ritual for banishing *lemures* from the home:

When midnight has come and lends silence to sleep, and dogs and all ye varied fowls are hushed, the worshipper who bears the olden rite in mind and fears the gods arises; no knots constrict his feet; and he makes a sign with his thumb in the middle of his closed fingers, lest in his silence an unsubstantial shade should meet him. And after washing his hands clean in spring water, he turns, and first he receives black beans and throws them away with face averted; but while he throws them, he says: 'These I cast; with these beans I redeem me and mine.' This he says nine times, without looking back: the shade is thought to gather the beans, and to follow unseen behind. Again he touches water, and clashes Temesan bronze, and asks the shade to go out of his house. When he has said nine times, 'Ghosts of my fathers, go forth!' he looks back, and thinks that he has duly performed the sacred rites.[5]

The laying of ghosts in the ancient world was sometimes far less genteel than a ritual involving a few beans. The Greeks, for example, practised something called 'armpitting'. Most famously committed by Clytemnestra against her husband, Agamemnon – whom she murdered on his return from the Trojan War – this procedure involved cutting off the extremities of the victim, stringing them together on a rope or band, and slinging this around the neck so the body parts dangled just below the victim's armpits. This was thought to hobble the ghost and prevent it from wreaking vengeance on its killer.

However, malignant ghosts could be put to effective use. In *Metamorphoses*, Apuleius tells the story of an angry wife who hires a witch to kill her husband; the witch calls up the spirit of a murdered woman and directs the ghost to the husband. The husband at first perceives the ghost as a living person – albeit a sickly and impoverished one – but the ghost vanishes and the husband is found dead by hanging (although it is never indicated whether homicide or suicide is the cause).

In the most famous and frequently repeated ghost story of the ancient world, a philosopher rents a house that is known to be haunted. In a version of the story by Pliny the Younger, the ghost is perhaps the first ever to be described as clanking chains (he is shackled around the hands and feet); in Lucian's version, the ghost transforms into various terrifying animals before being subdued by an Egyptian magic spell. In all tellings, the ghost leads the philosopher to a spot in the house; the next day it is dug up to reveal the spirit's long-forgotten corpse. Once the malevolent entity receives a proper burial, it disappears and the house is safe once more. (Some 1,500 years later, the sixteenth-century Spanish writer Antonio de Torquemada would recount a similar tale in his book *A Garden of Curious Flowers*: he describes the story of a young man named Vasquez de Ayola, who arrives in Bologna to study and rents a large house that is believed to be haunted. A month after his arrival, he is awakened one night by a hideous spectre bound in chains; the ghost leads him to a spot in the garden, and when that spot is dug up the following day an ancient corpse bound in chains is discovered. The haunting is ended, and Torquemada goes on to claim that witnesses to this event are still living.)

The historian Plutarch recounts (in his 'Life of Cimon') a tale of a haunted bath in his home town of Chæronea. Damon, an outlaw who slew Roman soldiers and laid waste to the country around the town, was lured by the city's inhabitants into the baths, where they waited until he was naked and being rubbed with oil to murder him. Afterwards there were so many frightful 'groaning and sighings' heard from the place that it was walled up, yet Plutarch tells us that 'terrible voices and cries' were still heard from the baths in his time.[6]

Although ghosts were frequently lethal to those mortals who encountered them, they were usually insubstantial and could neither touch nor be touched. An exception to this is found in *The Odyssey*; when Ulysses (or Odysseus) seeks the council of shades in Hades, he offers a black ram in sacrifice. When he sees the ghost of his own mother, Anticlea, she remains silent until she drinks the blood of the ram.

Even more blood-drenched is the second-century story of Polykritos, who dies four nights after taking a wife. Nine months later a hermaphroditic child is born to the woman, and the child becomes the subject of dispute among the local residents, since not only does it have two sets of genitals but its parents were on opposite sides of a political dispute. Suddenly the ghost of Polykritos appears, begging the citizens to allow it to take the child and end the dispute. As the townspeople argue, the spirit abruptly seizes the child and devours it except for the head; Polykritos then vanishes, but the child's disembodied head begins to speak, offering a doom-filled prophecy.

Occasionally these returning spirits engaged in so many physical acts – including carnal ones – that they must be thought of more as revenants than ghosts, since they clearly possessed bodies. The tale of Philinnion, from Phlegon's *Book of Marvels* (second century CE), indicates a revenant and possibly a *lamia*, a female vampire that fed on the blood of young men: the girl Philinnion is glimpsed by a maid in a room with a young man, Makhates, six months after her death. When the maid reports this to Philinnion's mother, the woman is sceptical and angry with the maid; by the time they return to Makhates' room, morning has arrived and the girl has vanished. The next night, however, she returns, and this time her parents confront her. They embrace her in astonishment, but she tells them she returned with divine help because of her passion for Makhates, and she immediately dies a second time. When the family tomb is opened, Philinnion's bier contains nothing but several objects belonging to Makhates. A local seer recommends that the girl's body be taken from the house and burned and that all who encountered her perform rituals to purify themselves; Makhates, however, despairs and commits suicide.

Given how often these returning spirits seem intent on causing harm to mortals, it is perhaps no surprise that the Romans had multiple holidays to appease and exorcise the dead. In addition to Lemuria, there was the nine-day celebration of Parentalia, held in February, which celebrated the ancestors by leaving offerings on their tomb. The climax of Parentalia was the gloomy midnight festival of Feralia, which was intended to pacify the more aggressive ghosts. In Book II of *Fasti*, Ovid describes a time when the Romans, preoccupied with war, forgot to honour their deceased kin:

> Once upon a time, waging long wars with martial arms, they did neglect the All Souls' Days. The negligence was not un-punished; for 'tis said that from that ominous day Rome grew hot with the funeral fires that burned without the city. They say, though I can hardly think it, that the ancestral souls did issue from the tombs and make their moan in the hours of stilly night; and hideous ghosts, a shadowy throng, they say, did howl about the city streets and the wide fields.[7]

The Greek poet and historian Hesiod, however, mentions a species of good ghosts (sometimes translated as 'good demons') that were the spirits of heroes or the 'golden race of mortal men'. These benevolent ghosts are 'keepers of mortal men; who watch over dooms and the sinful works of men, faring everywhere over the earth, cloaked in mist'.[8]

These heroic ghosts might appear to deliver warnings or prophecies. One of the best-known examples of this comes from Virgil's *Aeneid*, the great epic Latin poem written perhaps two decades before the birth of Christ. It follows Aeneas, a wanderer who survives the Trojan War and goes on to become the legendary ancestor of the Romans. In the second of the poem's twelve books, Aeneas is in Troy the night the city is fooled into taking in the Trojan Horse, and he is warned by the ghost of the great Trojan champion Hector, who endured a particularly gruesome death when he was dragged behind a carriage. Hector's shade appears before Aeneas, who notes that 'His hair and beard stood stiffen'd with his gore.'⁹ Hector goes on to suggest (albeit ambiguously) that Aeneas will be involved with the founding of Rome. Later, in Book VI, Aeneas enters a temple and begs the gods (by citing Orpheus, among others) to be allowed to descend into Hades and speak to his father. After sacrificing seven bulls, Aeneas is allowed to enter Hades, and much of the rest of this book describes the underworld, where Aeneas encounters vast woods, the great lake Acheron, terrifying mythological creatures (including Gorgons), Death and his 'half-brother, Sleep'. The temple priestess warns him that descending into Hades is easy, but the return trip is very difficult. Aeneas journeys through Hades, encountering the ghosts of friends who tell him of their deaths, and at last he finds Anchises, his father. He attempts three times to embrace his father, but 'thrice the flitting shadow slipp'd away.'¹⁰ Even in Hell, ghosts are too insubstantial to be grasped.

The theatre of the Greeks and Romans also reveals an interest in the shades of the dead, although perhaps more so with the Romans than the Greeks. Euripides, one of the most famed of the Greek playwrights, begins his *Hecuba* with a visit from the ghost of Polydorus, a young son of the king of Troy sent away for safe-keeping during the Trojan War to his father's friend Polymestor, with a small treasure; however, when Troy falls, Polymestor murders Polydorus for the treasure and casts his body into the sea. Without receiving a proper burial, Polydorus is doomed to haunt the Earth, and especially his mother, Hecuba. (Scholars continue to debate how the Greeks presented the ghosts on-stage; some have suggested that the shades were meant to appear elevated, possibly even on the roof of the theatre, while others believe that the verb used to suggest this elevation 'may be closer to the metaphorical English "in suspense" than literally "raised"'.¹¹) Later, the Roman playwright Pacuvius wrote his own version of Polydorus' tragedy in the play *Iliona*, of which only a few lines survive, including an especially poignant plea from the murdered hero's ghost for a proper burial. In yet another twist on this tale, Sophocles' play *Polyxena* (also in fragments) begins with the Greeks preparing to leave Troy after the war, only to be called back by the ghost of Achilles, which demands the sacrifice of the eponymous girl.

In Aeschylus' tragedy *The Persians*, the ghost of Darius is called back to Earth, and notes the difficulties involved:

> No light thing is it, to come back from death,
> For, in good sooth, the gods of nether gloom
> Are quick to seize but late and loth to free![12]

The Roman playwrights' shades seem more bloodthirsty than the Greeks', concerned more with wreaking havoc than with merely carrying out genteel hauntings until they received a proper burial. In Seneca's *Octavia*, the ghost of Agrippina sues for revenge:

> Among the dead
> The memory still lives of my foul murder,
> The infamous offence for which my ghost
> Still cries for vengeance.[13]

Similarly, in Seneca's tragedy *Thyestes*, Fury orders the ghost of Tantalus to return to Earth to create strife in the house of his grandson.

In Plautus' *Mostellaria* (*The Haunted House*), a ghost offers this dire speech:

> The King of Hades has refused to let me in
> Because I died . . . too early. And I was deceived
> By someone's word of honour. My host slaughtered me,
> And buried me in secret – here – unfuneralled.
> A sin. A sin for gold. Now, boy, move out of here!
> The house is full of sin, the habitation cursed.[14]

The surprise here, however, is that Plautus' play – considered by many critics to be his masterwork – is actually a comedy about a clever slave, Tranio, whose young master is hosting an amorous party when his father abruptly returns from a three-year absence. Tranio concocts the story that the house is haunted by a lethal spirit in order to keep the father out. *Mostellaria*, dating back to the second century BCE, is probably history's first well-known humorous ghost story.

At the northern end of the continent, the pantheistic Teutonic religions were also rich with ghost lore. Odin, the supreme god in Norse mythology, was sometimes called *Drauga Drott*, or 'lord of spectres', because of his ability to raise ghosts (*draugar*). The *draugar* and the *haugbúar* (barrow-dwelling ghosts) were fearsome creatures found in many of the sagas and the *Edda* of northern Europe. There were two types of *draugar*: the *Apturgöngur*, which returned from death of their own volition; and the *Uppvakníngar* ('up-awakened'), spirits called up by necromancers to do their bidding. The *Apturgön-gur* were usually associated with wealth; either they returned from the beyond to check on what they had left their heirs, or they occupied their graves intent on protecting the treasure with which they had been buried. The *Uppvakníngar* were said to exist for 120 years, growing in power during their first 40, retaining that power for the next 40 and then slowly ebbing away during the final four decades.

The *draugar* were anything but wispy spirits with little power; they were, instead, closer to revenants – reanimated corpses that could interact physically with mortal kin. These dead men were those who had been buried in barrows, and

> they frequently come out of their barrows, and walk, or even ride abroad ... This occurs most frequently in the evening, but it sometimes happens that a mist or temporary darkness her-alds their approach even by day. They are sometimes seen by the living in what appears to be a kind of dream or trance; but it generally happens even so that they leave beside the living person some gift, by which, on awakening, the living person may be assured of the tangible nature of the visit.[15]

The *haugbúi*, or 'barrow-dweller', was often associated with poetry, and might recite verses to those who wandered into or near its burial site. From the *Flateyjarbók* comes the story of a *haugbúi* named Thorleifr, who had been a great poet (*skald*) in the royal court of Denmark, until he had incurred the wrath of Jarl Hákon. The *jarl* enlisted the aid of magicians to create a wooden man who mortally wounded Thorleifr, and he was laid to rest in a barrow just north of the Hill of Laws. One day a shepherd named Hallbjörn fell asleep on the barrow while struggling with writing an ode to its occupant, and the ghost of Thorleifr came out of its barrow, took control of Hallbjörn's tongue and recited verses for him. When he woke, Hallbjörn remembered the poetry, and he soon became a great and much-admired *skald*.

The *draugar* and *haugbúi* were not always benevolent, however. The *Eyrbyggja Saga* offers the frightening story of Thorolf Twist-foot, whose ghost

> haunted these farms in such a violent fashion that no one would live there. Bolstad was now derelict, for once Arnkel was dead, Thorolf had begun to haunt there too, killing men and beasts alike, so that no one has ever had the courage to farm there since.[16]

In the *Laxdaela Saga*, the ghost of the ill-tempered Hrapp likewise returns to murder servants of his farm, until his body is dug up and moved far away. In *Grettir's Saga*, the hero fights with a *draugr* that rolls its eyes up under moonlight; the sight so disturbs Grettir that he remembers it for the rest of his life.

Many stories of fights with *draugar* involve heroes who are intent on claiming the creatures' treasures for themselves as well as on laying the ghosts, which could be achieved by entering the *draugr's* barrow and cutting off its head. This was especially dangerous if the *draugr* also employed *trollskap*, or evil magic, in guarding its barrow.

Not all the Scandinavian ghost stories were so violent or poetic. 'The Tale of Thorstein Shiver' (also from *Flateyjarbók*) takes a more humorous approach, offering the story of a trickster who triumphs over a *draugr*. Thorstein is in the party of King Olaf when he stops at a farm called Reim. As the evening's drinking festivities wind down, the king warns his men that none of them must venture out to the privy alone during the night. Thorstein awakens in the night with a need to relieve himself, disregards the king's warning and ventures to the outhouse, which is large enough to seat 22. After Thorstein settles himself, a ghost appears at the far end of the outhouse. The ghost identifies itself as Thorkel the Thin, and says it has just come up from Hell. Thorstein asks the ghost questions about Hell, and the demonic ghost answers, growing nearer to Thorstein throughout the conversation. Finally Thorstein asks Thorkel to re-create the loudest scream he has ever heard a victim utter in Hell, and the resulting sound causes Thorstein to lose consciousness. Just as Thorkel is about to descend on his victim, a bell rings and Thorstein is saved. Later on, he confesses his night-time indiscretion to King Olaf, who asks him why he wanted to hear the creature scream. Thorstein tells him that he knew Olaf would hear the sound and help, and Olaf admits that he rang the bell when he heard the scream. When Thorstein tells the king that the only fear he felt was a single shiver down his spine, Olaf dubs him Thorstein Shiver.[17]

Chapter 51 of *The Saga of the Ere-dwellers* tells the tale of a female Icelandic ghost. After she is caught in a rain of blood, Thorgunna becomes very ill, and on her deathbed she asks to be buried in distant Skalaholt. After her death, Goodman Thorod assembles a cadre of men and undertakes the journey. After travelling for many days they reach a place called Nether-ness and ask for shelter for the night, but the landowner refuses them food. As they settle down, hungry, to sleep, they hear a clatter in the kitchen; the landowner's men rush in to find a tall naked woman preparing a large meal. Thorod and his men recognize her as the late Thorgunna, and the landowner agrees to provide them with whatever they need. At that moment Thorgunna turns and walks out into the night, and is not seen again. However, when they reach Skalaholt, Thorgunna is once again in her coffin, and she is buried there according to her wishes.

As Christianity replaced the old pantheistic religions, common belief in ghosts did not abate, but took on new forms. Belief in spirits of the dead was tied to funerary rituals of the pagans, and ghosts – which were confined to Earth – clashed with the belief in other dwelling places for immortal souls. In Deuteronomy 18:10–11, Moses prohibits anyone who is 'a consulter with familiar spirits, or a wizard, or a necromancer', suggesting that communication with the dead and raising ghosts was considered possible. Also in the

Benjamin West, *Saul and the Witch of Endor*, late 18th century.

Bible, the Book of Leviticus warns against believing in mediums (or, as the King James translation phrases it, 'them that have familiar spirits'). The biblical scholar Deborah Thompson Prince has suggested that the resurrection of Jesus described in Luke 24 knowingly references different aspects of Greco-Roman ghost stories (the empty tomb of the revenant, the sudden appearance of the disembodied spirit, the revenant's ability to engage in eating) to express the truly unique nature of Jesus to an audience familiar with those old stories; or, as Prince puts it, 'to work within the parameters of the literary and cultural expectations of the audience to express a phenomenon that surpasses those expectations'.[18]

It was, however, the story of Saul, the Medium of Endor and the spirit of Samuel that would most clearly define early Christianity's views on ghosts. For centuries scholars argued the real nature of the spectre that appeared before Saul. Was it a revenant? A hallucination? A vision created by the medium? Satan himself? The twelfth-century theologian Peter Comestor suggested 'that with God's permission it was indeed the soul of Samuel, covered by a body, that appeared; but for others it was a body that was resuscitated and received the life of a spirit, while Samuel's soul remained in its resting place.'[19] A few centuries later, pictorial representations of the scene nearly always included Satan, suggesting that the diabolical deceit theory had won.

St Augustine (354–430 CE) led early Christian thought on ghosts; he did not dismiss the experience of those who encountered them, but neither did he believe them to be dead souls. Instead Augustine suggested that ghosts were spiritual visions planted by angels (or, should the encounter be fearful or otherwise negative, demons).

Eight centuries later, in his *Summa theologica* of about 1270, St Thomas argued that 'demons often pretend to be the souls of the dead, in order to confirm the error of heathen superstition.'[20] Thomas cites the story of Simon Magus, a legendary sorcerer who was said to have converted to Christianity in order to acquire the power of the Holy Ghost that came upon the Apostles, but the Apostles banished him from their company. In one of the many stories of sorcery surrounding Simon, he was said to have slain a boy and turned his ghost into a 'familiar spirit' that worked great magic. Thomas, however, argues that Simon was actually served by a demon masquerading as the spirit child.

A correspondent of St Augustine, Evodius, believed that ghosts could appear in dreams and convey messages to the living, and in one letter to Augustine he pondered the spirit of man:

> And I ask first whether there is a body that does not abandon the incorporeal reality, that is, the substance of the soul, when it leaves this earthly body, that is, either an airy or an ethereal body, if it is perhaps one of the four elements.[21]

Later on Evodius notes that 'the dead come, pay visits, and are seen outside of dreams.'[22]

Despite Augustine's thoughtful arguments and his popularity among Christian scholars, belief in ghosts during the first millennium CE did not abate, but if anything seemed to grow. Pope Gregory 1 – also known as Gregory the Great (540–604) – wrote frequently about ghosts in his *Dialogues*, and essentially created the model of the Christian ghost tale. In Gregory's accounts (which occupy a large portion of Book IV of the *Dialogues*), certain stories seem to focus on wraiths or fetches – a holy man's soul visits a brother monk at the time of his death, for example – but most record situations in which a dying man or woman receives a comforting visit from a saint. Chapter 12 of Book IV ('of the soul of Probus, Bishop of the City of Reati') offers the story of an elderly bishop, Probus, who has only a small boy for company on his deathbed:

> The little boy, standing by his bedside, suddenly saw certain men coming in to the man of God, apparelled in white stoles, whose faces were far more beautiful and bright than the whiteness of their garments: whereat being amazed and afraid, he began to cry out, and ask who they were: at which noise the Bishop also looking up, beheld them coming in and knew them, and thereupon comforted the little boy, bidding him not to cry, or be afraid, saying that they were the holy martyrs St Juvenal and St Eleutherius that came to visit him: but he, not acquainted with any such strange visions, ran out at the doors as fast as he could, carrying news hereof both to his father and the physicians; who, going down in all haste, found the Bishop departed: for those Saints, whose sight the child could not endure, had carried his soul away in their company.[23]

Not all Gregory's tales are so beatific, however. In Chapter 51 he describes a nun who was known for her 'ungracious and foolish tongue'; after her death she is buried in the church, but the following night the keeper sees her body brought before the altar and cut in half, with one side being burned. The next morning he shows others the burn marks on the marble, and they realize that even being buried in church will not excuse all sins.[24]

Five centuries later, another Christian scribe would also describe a gruesome burning at an altar. The eleventh-century bishop Thietmar of Merseburg wrote extensively about both the military history of the Holy Roman Empire and ghost stories. Thietmar's *Chronicon* tells of singing figures heard (and glimpsed) in graveyards, and – in one exceptionally frightening instance – of a gathering of the dead in a reconstructed church; on the third night of their appearance, they subdue the local priest and burn him alive on the altar of the church. Thietmar's niece Brigida recalls this particular tale, and concludes by noting: 'As the day to the living, so the night is conceded to the dead.'[25]

To Thietmar, ghosts are perfectly aligned with Scripture. In Chapter 11 of Book 1 of his *Chronicon*, Thietmar begins a ghost story by telling us 'that no one faithful to Christ may doubt the future resurrection of the dead'; in Chapter 13, he states: 'I have written these things which happened in our most recent times so that the incredulous may learn that the words of the prophets are true.'[26] He goes on to quote Scripture, such as Isaiah 26:19 ('Thy dead men shall live, together with my dead body shall they arise'), to support his belief in ghosts, and to suggest that they serve a purpose: they return to offer signs about coming events.

By the end of the twelfth century, the English historian William of Newburgh pondered the large number of reports of ghost sightings, which he compared to what he thought was a relatively small number reported by 'the Ancients'. He noted that he could not record every report he heard because his 'task would be much too great and weighty'.[27]

Ghost stories were frequently collected by monasteries, where they served to prove the existence of the afterlife and the possibility of miracles. These tales – which usually centred on the spirits of saints or monks – might tell of a troubled spirit returning to seek masses or prayers, a ghost providing some form of instruction or a supernatural visitor offering descriptions of the angels, the Virgin Mary or Heaven. One holiday even resulted from such a tale: when Odilo, head of the abbey at Cluny in eastern France, heard of demons in crevices of Mount Etna wailing about losing souls to the powerful suffrages performed by the Cluniac monks, he instituted All Souls' Day on 2 November (following All Saints' Day on 1 November). All Souls' Day – during which believers pray for the souls of loved ones to be released from Purgatory – may have provided some of the more macabre elements of the modern celebration of Halloween, or the eve of All Saints' (or Hallows') Day.

Not all religious scholars thought that spirits returning to beg for masses or prayers were a sign of divine good. Writing in 1759, the Benedictine monk Dom Augustin Calmet argued that

> it is not an uncommon thing for the soul of some wicked wretch, or the devil in the shape of such a one, to come and desire masses, in order to have it thought, that he is in purgatory, and by this means, to possess others with a groundless and even dangerous hope of being saved, notwithstanding their wicked lives, and impenitent deaths.[28]

Possession of a human body is not confined solely to demons or the Devil, for the broader term of 'evil spirits' may include malevolent ghosts. In his book *The Spirits of Darkness* (1889), the Reverend John Gmeiner suggests three manners by which evil spirits may seek to control humans: 'invasion' is the temporary control of all or part of a human body by a supernatural force; 'obsession' calls for spirits to surround a human; and 'possession' involves permanent control of a human body and the use of all its organs and limbs.[29] The difficulty in distinguishing between a demon and a ghost in cases of possession was made most clear by a famous case from the sixteenth century. On All Souls' Day in 1565, a French girl named Nicola Aubry was praying at the grave of her grandfather, who had died about two years earlier, when the apparition of a figure covered in a white shroud appeared and said: 'I am your grandfather.'[30] It appeared again five days later, this time showing its face and telling the terrified teenager that it was in Purgatory. Soon, Nicola began to exhibit classic signs of possession: impossible strength, knowledge of events that were occurring far away, and the ability to speak and understand languages she had never studied. She eventually claimed to be possessed by 'Beelzebub', as well as an astonishing 29 other evil spirits. Her exorcism eventually took place in the cathedral at Laon, where 150,000 people were said to have witnessed strange phenomena during the rite. Finally, three months after the onset of possession, the spirit controlling Nicola gave a last burst of superhuman strength and vanished in a clap of thunder and a cloud of smoke. What the many glorious Catholic accounts of this possession fail to mention is that the possession and exorcism took place during a time of strife between French Catholics and Protestants, and most Protestants believed the entire incident to be a hoax perpetrated to advance the cause of Catholicism.

In those areas of Europe known as the 'Six Celtic Nations' – Wales, Scotland, Brittany, Ireland, the Isle of Man and Cornwall – early ghost stories were less likely to include a Christian aspect, but might instead focus on a prominent figure who is a sort of ghost ruler. In Brittany – where in the twelfth and thirteenth centuries tall conical towers called *lanternes des morts* (lanterns of the dead) were built in cemeteries, possibly to light the cemeteries at night as defence against wandering ghosts – legends abound of the Ankou, described variously as a personification of Death or as a local ruler of the dead who is replaced each year by the last person to die in that parish. 'Hellequin's Hunt' originated in ancient Germany, and found its way to Britain as 'the Wild Hunt', 'Herne the Hunter' or 'Gabriel Ratchets'. In its most basic form, it consists of a procession of spirits on horseback, usually witnessed by a single traveller in an isolated location; the parade may include knights and soldiers – some of whom may be known to the living witness – or may be a more ferocious collection of hunters and hounds. The first such description came from a monk in the year 1091, and the Hunt has been seen hundreds of times since. Shakespeare mentions Herne the Hunter in *The Merry Wives of Windsor*, and a description from 1874 describes him as 'the ghostly Hunter, on his barebacked steed, surrounded by his demon crew and his gaunt black hounds ... in his deer-skin garb, and antlered helm, his clanking chain and enchanted hunting-horn, out of which he had the power of blowing volumes of sulphureous vapour.'[31] Herne was thought to have been a woodman who, having fallen into disgrace, hanged himself from an oak tree in Windsor forest in the fourteenth century; although the particular tree – known as 'Herne's Oak' – was destroyed in a storm in 1863, his ghost is still thought to haunt that area, and has been seen before catastrophic events, including the start of the Second World War. Locals have described auditory encounters that are typical for those haunted by a version of the Wild Hunt: they sometimes hear the baying of hounds and the sound of galloping horses' hooves.

*Chambers's Encyclopaedia* states that the Wild Hunt represents

> the Christian degradation of the old heathen gods. Like Woden, the lord of all atmospheric and weather phenomena, and consequently of storms, the Wild Huntsman also appears on horseback in hat and cloak, accompanied by a train of spirits – by the ghosts of drunkards, suicides, and other malefactors, often without heads, or otherwise mutilated.[32]

As Gabriel Ratchets (or Gabble Rachets), the huntsman is said to be heard leading his spectral hounds high overhead, condemned to an eternal airborne hunt for the sin of having hunted on a Sunday. In Ireland, the 'Dead Hunt' was known to residents of the Lough Gur area, who claimed to hear the dogs' panting tongues along with their pounding paws. Locals believed that only the elderly heard the Hunt.

In Scotland and Ireland, fairies were often allied with ghosts, and in some stories the two seem to be interchangeable. The Irish Celts once celebrated their new year, Samhain (the ancestor of the modern Halloween), on 31 October; although this was a day marked by financial and agricultural tasks (collecting tax, bringing livestock in from the fields for winter, and so on), it was also a night when the veil between our world and others was believed to be at its thinnest. Although Celtic tales have a surprising dearth of ghosts, malevolent *sidh* (fairies) are in abundance and might cross over on Samhain Eve to attack humans. The melding of ghosts with fairies features more prominently in later Irish tales, such as 'The Dance of the Dead', collected by Lady Wilde in *Ancient Legends, Mystic Charms and Superstitions of Ireland* of 1887 (oddly, this passage suggests that the most dangerous time is actually not the first night of November, but the last):

It is especially dangerous to be out late on the last night of November, for it is the closing scene of the revels – the last night when the dead have leave to dance on the hill with the fairies, and after that they must all go back to their graves and lie in the chill, cold earth, without music or wine till the next November comes round, when they all spring up again in their shrouds and rush out into the moonlight with mad laughter.[33]

The story goes on to tell of a woman who, out late on a November night, encounters a dead man she once knew. He shows her a host of the dead dancing on a hillside, then warns her to run lest the fairies arrive and force her to join the dance. Unfortunately, before she can escape the fairies form a ring around her; although she awakens in her own bed, she dies a few days later of 'fairy-stroke' and does indeed join the dance.

There is certainly no ghost associated with 31 October that is more well-known, however, than Jack-o'-Lantern. Jack's origins lie in the legends of the *ignis fatuus* (Latin for 'foolish fire') or swamp gas that forms from the natural decomposition of organic materials in marshy areas and produces a faint bluish glow. Also known as will-o'-the-wisp, *ignis fatuus* was usually thought to be ghostly, and some were even believed to lead unwary travellers over the edge of cliffs or into deadly areas of the swamp. In Scandinavia, seizing a will-o'-the-wisp would leave the journeyer holding a bone; in other areas, it was believed that the glow was encased in a skeletal rib-cage. Offering a small sacrifice to the spirit – a coin or a crumb of food – might protect the traveller from mischief and provide safe passage home.

Given the marsh lights' propensity for deceiving those who encountered them, they soon gained the reputation of being trick-sters, and an entire cycle of trickster legends sprang up around them. Since those who met the lights while staggering through a bog at night were often returning home from a tavern, Jack (or Will) became the spirit of a man who had wallowed in drunkenness, and his legends are told all over Europe. In early versions, the trickster is a good-natured innkeeper who plays host to Christ and his disciples, and in return is granted three wishes. When he finally dies, he is on his way to Paradise when he passes the gates of Hell, where he engages in a card game with the Devil, wagering his own soul against the release of a number of others. The innkeeper wins, and gains admission to Heaven for those whose souls he has freed.

In the later, more traditional versions of the story, however, Jack is a clever but debauched blacksmith whose soul the Devil arrives one day to claim. Three times Jack tricks the Devil out of taking him, and Jack always plans repentance, but fails to follow through. When he runs out of time and finally dies, Jack finds that neither Heaven nor Hell wants him; the Devil, however, grants him a burning ember from the fires of Hell to light his way, and Jack places the ember in a hollowed-out gourd or turnip (or, in American versions, a pumpkin). His spirit then wanders the Earth eternally, lit by the glowing light from his lantern, causing mischief in swamps and marshes.

It is difficult to say exactly when Jack's legend became entwined with Halloween; in the New World, for instance, jack-o'-lanterns were not associated with the festival until the end of the nineteenth century. However, there is no question that the holiday has always had a close association with spirits of the dead, and as such is similar to celebrations found around the world that honour the ghosts of ancestors and invite them to return home. Halloween derives from the celebration of All Saints' Day on 1 November (a date probably chosen in an attempt by the Catholic Church to co-opt celebrations of Samhain), but in the eleventh century Catholics began to celebrate All Souls' Day on 2 November, to honour their own deceased loved ones. In many areas of Europe, it was customary to leave food and drink out during this time, since the spirits were thought to return home (possibly released from Purgatory for a single night); in this respect, the celebration is similar to the Chinese Hungry Ghost Festival, the Mexican *Dias de los Muertos* and other festivals that honour and propitiate the ghosts of ancestors. Although few European countries continue the practice of leaving out food, many still mark 1 November by visiting cemeteries to clean and decorate the graves of loved ones. And Halloween, of course, has retained a strong association with ghosts; the image of the white-sheeted spirit has become one of the festival's main icons, alongside the jack-o'-lantern.

Throughout history, hauntings have sometimes served as a sort of metaphysical conscience, re-enacting some infamous tragedy that retains its vitality as a ghost story. Take, for example, the tragic death of 150 Jews at Clifford's Tower in York: in March 1190, a wave of anti-Semitism swept through England, and in York many of the town's Jewish population took refuge in Clifford's Tower, once the keep of York Castle and still an impressive construction, built

Halloween postcard showing a ghost with a jack-o'-lantern head, c. 1910.

Halloween
pranksters
encounter a
real ghost on
this postcard,
c. 1915.

HALLOWEEN GREETINGS

on a motte overlooking the city. A siege ensued, and on 16 March, realizing there was no escape, the Jews in the tower chose instead to take their own lives. Not long thereafter, reports began to surface that the tower's stones bled each year on 16 March. Although the walls have not been seen bleeding for some time, the tower is still a featured spot on ghost tours and the subject of paranormal investigations.

On the far side of the world, America's many indigenous peoples had a variety of ghost beliefs. Most Native American tribes practised some form of animism, and so ascribed spirits not only to themselves but also to other animals. Extensive rituals honoured

Interior of Clifford's Tower in York.

the spirits of larger prey – especially bears – as they were killed, skinned and consumed; the animals were often given titles such as 'Grandfather'. To the Navajos of the southwestern United States, ghosts were terrifying creatures called *chindi*. The good parts of the deceased moved on, but the evil parts were left behind as *chindi*, which could cause sickness or death to those unlucky enough to encounter them. Because *chindi* might linger where the owner's death had occurred, Navajos abandoned any house or *hogan* where someone had died, and they avoided ever speaking a dead person's name. A ritual called the Enemy Way could exorcise a *chindi*, but these malevolent spirits could also be called and controlled by skilled medicine men. One *chindi* story centred on a family, the Long Salts, who had once engaged a medicine man to perform a healing. As part of his payment, the medicine man had asked for five butchered sheep; however, since the medicine man was blind, one of the Long Salts tried to deceive him by offering five antelope instead. The medicine man called forth a *chindi*, and one of the Long Salt family mysteriously fell sick and died. The Long Salts tried to return to the medicine man to ask him to call off the vengeful spirit, but he died before they could reach a deal, and within a few years the *chindi* had hunted down all the Long Salts except a sixteen-year-old girl. She was taken in by a trader named Behegade who thought he could escape from the *chindi*, and for a short time he was successful, but soon the winter snow set in and slowed them down. The *chindi* caught up with the girl and she died in one night.[34]

Not all Native American ghosts were vindictive, however. The Potawatomi tribe of the Great Lakes told of a poor, orphaned hunter who encountered two ghosts one night while encamped in an old, forgotten burial ground. The hunter greeted the ghosts and offered prayers and food for them; the next day, he was rewarded with luck and hunting success (he killed four bucks). Upon returning to his village, he consulted an elder, who told him this was a good omen and urged him to hold a feast for his two unearthly visitors. The poor man went on to become a great hunter who 'never forgot to sacrifice holy tobacco to the two spirits'.[35]

Ghost stories are rare – if not truly non-existent – in the classical literature of Arabic nations. One story in the *Arabian Nights*, 'Ali the Cairene and the Haunted House in Baghdad', concerns a house that is occupied by a *jinn* (or *djinn*), a spirit born of 'smokeless fire' that ends up offering young Ali (who has just arrived from Cairo) not a fright, but rather a fortune in gold. (The jinn has, however, slain all previous occupants of the house, since the gold was intended only for Ali.) In the annotations to his translation of *Arabian Nights*,

A magician raises a ghost in this 16th-century illustration from *The Red Dragon*.

Richard Burton notes that in the Middle East, 'haunted houses are ... tenanted by Ghuls, Jinns and a host of supernatural creatures; but not by ghosts proper.'[36]

A remarkable ordinance from 1284 suggests that there was a strong belief at this time not only in ghosts, but also in human abilities to call them forth. The English Guilds were essentially neighbourhood benevolent societies that provided support to their members, and each Guild issued its own set of rules. Ludlow's Guild of the Palmers stipulated this: 'If any man wishes, as is common, to keep night-watches with the dead, this will be allowed, on the condition that he neither calls up ghosts, nor makes any mockeries of the body or its good name, nor does any other scandal of the kind.'[37]

A spell book of 1521, *The Red Dragon* (also known as *The Grand Grimoire*), does indeed contain instructions for raising ghosts. It begins: 'It is absolutely necessary to assist at the Christmas Mass, at precisely midnight, in order to have a familiar conversation with the inhabitants of the other world.' The magician is instructed to pronounce the phrase '*Exsurgent mortui et ad me veniunt*' ('Rise up, dead one, and indeed come to me') during the Mass, then proceed to the graveyard, where prayers are said and rituals conducted. Among the elaborate proceedings, two bones must be thrown at a temple; the magician must walk 'four miles, nineteen hundred steps' to the east; and when the spectre appears, the necromancer must say '*Ego sum te peto et videre queto*' ('I am requesting to be able to see you').[38]

# 3
# Rattling Chains and White Sheets: Ghosts in the Western World

As Europe moved out of the Dark Ages – the centuries of feudalism, plague and superstitious beliefs that resulted in the deaths of tens of thousands of people accused of witchcraft – a new wave of philosophers and scientists re-examined the world around them, including ghosts. After centuries of being affiliated with religion and magic, ghosts entered the secular realm.

One of the first plays of the modern era, and in addition one of the first revenge plays, Thomas Kyd's *The Spanish Tragedy* (written sometime between 1582 and 1592) remains firmly rooted in classical mythology and owes much to Seneca. It begins with the ghost of Don Andrea being denied passage by Hades' ferryman, Charon, until he receives a proper burial. Compare this with Shakespeare's *Hamlet*, which was written a few years later and first published in 1603: the latter by and large removes mythology and religion from the ghost equation, using the ghost of Hamlet's father instead as an engine of revenge. The ghost is first dismissed by Horatio as 'but our fantasy', then it appears to Hamlet and tells him:

> I am thy father's spirit,
> Doom'd for a certain term to walk the night,
> And for the day confined to fast in fires,
> Till the foul crimes done in my days of nature
> Are burnt and purged away. (1.5)

The ghost's speech suggests that he languishes in Purgatory and that his soul may be redeemed, but explicit references are notably missing.

The thinkers of the Age of Enlightenment were even more dismissive of ghosts. In 1674 the great Dutch philosopher Baruch Spinoza, responding to a letter that inquired about his opinion of ghosts, wrote:

> To confess the truth, I have never read a trustworthy author, who clearly showed that there are such things ... What are these ghosts or spectres? Are they children, or fools, or madmen? For all that I have heard of them seems more adapted to the silly than the wise, or, to say the best we can of it, resembles the pastimes of children or of fools.[1]

Thomas Hobbes, the English philosopher credited with being among the first to emphasize liberal notions of equality and individual rights, equated ghosts with what he believed to be antiquated practices in Catholicism:

> From this ignorance of how to distinguish dreams, and other strong fancies, from vision and sense, did arise the greatest part of the religion of the Gentiles in time past, that worshipped satyrs, fauns, nymphs, and the like; and nowadays the opinion that rude [primitive] people have of fairies, ghosts, and goblins ... And for fairies, and walking ghosts, the opinion of them has, I think, been on purpose either taught, or not confuted, to keep in credit the use of exorcism, of crosses, of holy water, and other such inventions of ghostly men.[2]

As the witch persecution of the previous century began to ebb, along with belief in such creatures as fairies (now reduced almost literally to mere 'fairy tales'), ghost sightings changed in character, but did not diminish in number reported; in fact, if anything there seemed to be more encounters with spirits and apparitions. As with Shakespeare's ghosts, the real-life reports no longer centred on active monasteries or temples, but instead were often near ruins of such structures. Perhaps the new ghosts of the Enlightenment represented our fears about the Dark Ages we had only recently escaped.

Between 1600 and 1847 – the era before the spread of Spiritualism through both the Old World and the New – stories of hauntings proliferated throughout Europe and especially Britain, with several cases becoming so well-known that they spawned books and trials, and are still studied by modern paranormal experts. The first is known as 'The Glanvill Narrative' or, more commonly, 'The Drummer of Tedworth'. The case occupied the English press for nearly twenty years, probably thanks to its promotion by an author who was religious, educated and distantly connected to royalty.

The Reverend Joseph Glanvill was chaplain-in-ordinary to Charles II; he was also a member of the Royal Society, and possessed an interest in the occult. His book *Saducismus triumphatus*, published in 1666 under a different title and then posthumously in 1681, was a collection of stories of witches and apparitions, most of which Glanvill had collected via hearsay. However, the first tale in the book, 'The Dæmon of Tedworth', told of a haunting that Glanvill claimed to have witnessed parts of. The story began in 1661, when the magistrate John Mompesson ordered the arrest of a drummer named William Drury who had attempted to use counterfeit notes with a local constable. The constable relieved Drury of his drum, which he eventually sent to the magistrate's house. Soon afterwards the house was besieged with loud thumps and raps, coming from the doors, walls and even the roof. The sounds continued for months, and then the activity focused on the Mompesson children, who claimed not simply to hear the drumming sounds, but also to be touched and even lifted by unseen hands. Movement of objects became commonplace – 'the chairs walkt about the room of themselves' – and the poundings would occasionally echo other sounds or seem to be offered in answer to questions.

Glanvill first visited the Mompesson house in January 1662, during which time he heard scratching noises in the children's

The Drummer of Tedworth, from the frontispiece
to the third edition of *Saducismus triumphatus* (1700).

bedroom that he could not explain, and an animalistic panting. The
disturbances continued for two years and were witnessed by numerous guests; even Mompesson's attempt to arrest the drummer for
witchcraft (he was found not guilty) failed to halt the cacophony.
At one point Mompesson was quoted as saying he had 'found the
trick', but he later denied any imposture himself or the discovery
of any hoax.

The Drummer of Tedworth inspired controversy for decades.
A number of histories and treatises on ghosts dismissed it as a hoax.
It inspired a ballad – Abraham Miles's 'A Wonder of Wonders;
Being a True Relation of the Strange and Invisible Beating of a
Drum, at the House of John Mompeson [*sic*], Esquire, at Tidcombe
[*sic*] in the County of Wilt-shire', published in 1663 – one comedic
play, Joseph Addison's *The Drummer, or the Haunted-house* (1716);

William Hogarth, *Credulity, Superstition and Fanaticism: A Medley*, 1762.

and part of a famed satirical print by William Hogarth, *Credulity, Superstition and Fanaticism: A Medley* (1762), which mocks religious fervour and gullibility by putting the Drummer and other famous spirits in the middle of a church during a sermon delivered by a preacher wielding puppets of a witch and a devil.

In researching the story of the Drummer, including studying letters written by and to Mompesson and Glanvill, the historian Michael Hunter uncovered additional background to the case, including Mompesson's anxiety and Glanvill's literary embellishment of certain aspects. Hunter has suggested that this poltergeist tale serves as a sort of transition from earlier modes of thought to Restoration thinking:

> Having started as a symptom of the anxious, perplexed world of the early Restoration – the world of the Mirabilis Annus tracts – it then acquired a new dimension due to the input of the tropes of demonology and of fairy beliefs.[3]

Fifty years after the Drummer, another poltergeist case became famous for both its credibility (many witnesses recorded the same phenomena occurring at the same times) and one of its central figures: John Wesley, the founder of Methodism. Wesley's father, Samuel Wesley, was rector of Epworth in Lincolnshire. On the evening of 2 December 1716, two servants in the household heard strange knocking, saw floating objects and were distressed by the sound of a turkey gobbling near a bed. Over the next two months, the Wesley household was plagued with knocking and the sound of footfalls, silk rustling, glass bottles breaking and tinkling metal coins. The Wesley children became so accustomed to their super-natural visitor that they named it 'Old Jeffrey'; however, when the unknown entity persisted in frightening them and the family dog, Samuel challenged it to join him in his study, where he attempted unsuccessfully to communicate with it. Although the activity ceased in late January 1717, John Wesley's sister Emily reported the presence of 'Old Jeffrey' in a letter to her brother written 35 years later.

The Epworth story, as it is commonly known, includes an interesting political side. There was speculation that the ghost had come as a result of Mrs Wesley's refusal to say 'Amen' at the end of prayers for King William, whom she did not support. However, Samuel Taylor Coleridge, in his annotations for Robert Southey's *Life of Wesley*, found it more likely that the Wesleys suffered from 'a contagious nervous disease'.[4]

Daniel Defoe, the author of *Robinson Crusoe*, may have both created the modern era's first great ghost hoax and demonstrated the commercial potential for ghost stories when he was asked in 1706 to contribute a new introduction to the fourth edition of a religious work. Charles Drelincourt was a well-regarded Protestant theologian whose *Christians Defence Against the Fears of Death* (1651) was translated into English several decades later, but failed to produce significant sales. The publisher, a Mr Midwinter, asked Defoe to provide a new preface to the work, and Defoe thus produced 'A True Relation of the Apparition of Mrs Veal, Next Day After her Death, to One Mrs Bargrave, at Canterbury, on the 8th of September, 1705; which Apparition Recommends the Perusal of Drelincourt's Book of Consolation Against the Fears of Death'. The essay relates the story of Mrs Bargrave, who one day about noon received a visit from her friend, Mrs Veal. The latter lady was dressed in a riding habit, as if about to embark on a trip, and refused to kiss her friend in their usual fashion. The visit lasted just over 90 minutes before Mrs Veal departed. Later, Mrs Bargrave found out that her friend had truly departed that day at noon precisely, in Dover, some 20 miles away.

George Cruikshank's engraving showing the discovery of a cellar spirit, 1864.

After the addition of this preface, the sales of Drelincourt's book improved tremendously. Unfortunately, the tale was somewhat less than a 'true relation': 'It had all along been known to the literary world that this "*true* relation" was a "*falsehood*"', said the famed illustrator George Cruikshank in his humorous book *A Discovery Concerning Ghosts*.[5] In the same book, Cruikshank offers an amusing exposé of a haunted cellar tale:

> In the wine cellar of a wealthy gentleman's estate near Blackheath, a variety of sounds – groaning, knockings, footsteps – were said to be heard late at night, and finally the gentleman decided to solve the mystery of his haunting. One night, when the sounds were heard, he quickly assembled a small armed party and descended into the cellar. Nothing was to be seen there, and all was quiet except a strange, smothered kind of sound, like the hard breathing of an animal, something like snoring, that seemed to proceed out of the earth in one of the dark corners of the vault, when, lo and behold! In turning their lights in the direction from which the sounds came, and advancing carefully, they discovered – what do you think? Don't be alarmed. Why, the ghost lying on the ground, dead – DRUNK! Yes, the ghost had *laid* himself, not with 'Bell, Book and Candle', but by swallowing the SPIRIT of ALCOHOL, the spirit of wine, beer, and brandy. Most disgraceful; in fact, this ghost had taken a '*drop too much*'.[6]

The most famous spirit imposture of all time is undoubtedly the Cock Lane Ghost, a tale that easily rivals the popularity of the Drummer of Tedworth, despite a decidedly earthbound conclusion. This London haunting was so famous that Charles Dickens referred to it in several of his novels (including the beginning of *A Tale of Two Cities*), and, as Horace Walpole (whose novel *The Castle of Otranto* started the Gothic literature cycle), noted in a letter of 1762, 'the whole town of London think[s] of nothing else.'[7] In 1759 a widower and moneylender named William Kent moved to London with his late wife's sister, Fanny; Fanny and William had begun a romantic relationship, but were prevented from marrying by canon law. They stayed at a house on Cock Lane owned by Richard Parsons, where Fanny slept with Parsons's eleven-year-old daughter, Elizabeth. Not long afterwards they moved to new lodgings, but Fanny died shortly thereafter from smallpox, leaving Kent to inherit her estate. It wasn't long before the haunting began in earnest, when Elizabeth and another child with whom she now slept reported hearing knocking and scratching beneath their bed. Soon, sightings of an apparition were reported, an apparition that bore the likeness of Fanny, glowed with an intense light and beckoned to one man in a nearby pub. Rumours of murder began to surface; had Kent first seduced the naive Fanny and then slain her to obtain her money? Parsons had borrowed money from Kent, which he had repaid only when legal action was threatened, and meanwhile some of Fanny's relatives began to question her will – why had they inherited nothing?

When Parsons's daughter began to have fits, some suspected that Fanny's spirit had taken possession of her. A clergyman was brought in to examine the girl, and under questioning she revealed that she was indeed Fanny, that Kent had poisoned her and that she desired to see him hanged. The spirit communicated via knocks (one for yes, two for no) and scratching (to indicate displeasure generally), and a fluttering sound was said to be heard around the room when it arrived and departed.

'Scratching Fanny' became the rage of London. Crowds filled Cock Lane, making it frequently impassable. It was mocked by the likes of Samuel Johnson, parodied in faux playbills and ridiculed by any number of sceptics, yet it continued to hold sway over the public imagination. In an effort to investigate further, the child was removed to the house of a local rector, where the spirit was questioned, to no avail. Kent himself paid Elizabeth a visit, and when the spirit failed to answer questions, he was told it would not appear in the company of disbelievers; however, after being asked to leave the room for a few moments, he was readmitted and the knocks began. Finally a trip was made to Fanny's coffin, for the spirit had promised to knock from within, but no such proof was obtained: the coffin remained silent.

During one final investigation, as the knocks and scratching were heard again, a maid testified that a small board used in the kitchen was missing, and when the child was searched the board was discovered in her bed. In July 1762 the matter went to court, where five people were found guilty in a conspiracy, including a maid, a parson and a neighbour who had all participated in the hoax. Parsons, his wife and the maid went to prison, while the other two paid significant sums to Kent.

The Cock Lane Ghost – which concerns in part an impover-ished parish clerk with a drinking problem (Parsons) – did nothing to abate belief or interest in ghost stories. If anything, it made those that featured witnesses from professions considered to be rational or honest – clergymen, judges, doctors or military men – even more popular than they had been in the past. Take, for example, the case of the haunted castle of Slawensik, in Upper Silesia. In November 1806 a councillor named Hahn, who was attached to the prince's court, and a Prussian soldier named Kern arrived at the castle, where Hahn was told to await orders from the prince. On the third night of their stay, large pieces of lime began to fall around them; within a

MISS FANNY'S THEATRE,
IN COCK-LANE.

BY PARTICULAR DESIRE OF SEVERAL PERSONS OF QUALITY,
To-Morrow Evening, being the 16th inst.,
WILL BE PERFORMED AN ENTERTAINMENT OF
SCRATCHING AND KNOCKING,
OF THREE ACTS,
EACH TO CONCLUDE WITH A FLUTTER.
To begin precisely at 12 o'clock.
Beds, 10s. 6d. ; Chairs, 5s. ; Standing, 2s. 6d.
☞ No money to be returned after the first scratch, and nothing under the full price will be taken.

Satirical handbill for the Cock Lane Ghost.

few more nights, their attempts to sleep were continually interrupted by loud pounding and drumming. They sent for a local woman who possessed keys to the castle and searched all its rooms thoroughly, but found nothing. Soon objects were flying around them, witnessed by Hahn's retinue and other visitors to the castle. One night Kern glanced into a mirror and saw the transparent figure of a woman reflected there; he watched it for ten minutes, trying to ascertain whether it was real or illusory, until he saw its eyes move. A visiting Bavarian officer named Magerle, on being left alone in the room in which the worst of the disturbances had occurred, became so enraged by being pelted with flying objects that he drew his sabre and stabbed repeatedly into the air around him. Kern and Hahn endured this activity for two months, until Kern's favourite clay pipe was broken, the activity ceased and they left the castle. Nearly a quarter of a century after these events, a gentleman visited Slawensik for the purposes of investigating Hahn's narrative; he was informed that the castle had been destroyed, but that a man's skeleton had been found walled up in the ruins, the skull split open, presumably by the sword found near the body.

In *Fallacy of Ghosts, Dreams, and Omens* (1848), Charles Ollier offers a ghost story that sheds some light on why hauntings so often occur in old, dilapidated structures. He recounts the tale of a military man who took possession of a haunted castle that was the source of strange and terrifying sounds. When the wailing began in the middle of the night, he followed it down to the great hall, and discovered that parts of an ancient chapel organ had been used to shore up repairs done a century before; when the wind blew through the castle's many nooks, it was sometimes funnelled through the old organ pipes.[8] No doubt many haunted sites were imbued with similar ancient architectural oddities that created sounds or sights that were easily mistaken as belonging to another world.

A remarkable tale from the New World attests to how poltergeists crossed the Atlantic with their mortal friends. In the summer of 1797 a Catholic priest, Father Gallitzin, was sent to investigate a haunting in rural Virginia. A Lutheran farmer named Adam Livingston had taken in a poor Irish Catholic traveller, who had died while in Livingston's care. The Lutherans had provided every kindness for the Irishman, except that an unreasonable fear of Catholic priests kept them from honouring the dying man's wish of seeing a priest. Shortly thereafter the Livingstons' farm was the site of a spectacular haunting, witnessed by many:

> his barns got on fire and burned down, nobody knew how; his horses and cattle died; his clothing and those of his family, their beds and bedding were either burnt up, or cut into strips so small they could never be mended or put together again, generally in little pieces in the shape of a crescent.[9]

One elderly lady, intrigued by the stories of the clipping, went to the house with a new black silk hat in her pocket, carefully wrapped. After she left the house, she withdrew the parcel, pulled back the wrapping and found the hat sliced to ribbons. News of the haunting became so widespread that the location even acquired a new name: Cliptown. After having a dream about a Catholic priest, Livingston sent for Father Gallitzin, who with the aid of a second priest was able to expel whatever presence had invaded the house. The story has a final, odd ghostly twist: after converting to Catholicism, Livingston experienced visions in which he essentially received instruction in the mysteries of his new faith, and many believed these visions were a soul from Purgatory reaching out to the converted farmer.

A particularly crafty spirit (or *Klopfgeist*, in the original German) was encountered in about 1850 in the Germantown area of Wisconsin. A priest named Francis Xavier Paulhuber visited a house that was said to be haunted; the cautious Father took with him a party of strong, fearless men, but they soon encountered such baffling occurrences that several of them began to suspect witches. The spirit rapped out a message on a table in which it stated that the good priest himself had summoned it in order to make money from expelling it. Father Paulhuber suffered considerable persecution thereafter.[10]

No nineteenth-century American ghost would become as famous as the Bell Witch. One day in 1817 a Tennessee farmer and

Baptist elder, John Bell, spotted a strange animal in his fields, something he described as having the body of a dog and the head of a rabbit. The animal disappeared, but other weird phenomena began: rapping, scratching sounds on bedposts and covers being pulled from the beds of the Bell children. Many of the happenings surrounded the teenage Betsy, who was slapped and pinched. The spirit voice grew louder, singing hymns and repeating sermons. Word of the supernatural goings-on at the Bell farm spread to Nashville, where Major-General Andrew Jackson took an interest and decided to pay the Bells a visit. When his carriage stuck upon arrival on the outskirts of the Bell property, Jackson said to his men that it must be the Bell Witch, and the carriage was abruptly freed to move again. A 'witch tamer' in Jackson's entourage threatened the spirit with a silver bullet, at which point he was slapped and kicked from the house. Jackson wanted to stay to expose what he believed to be fraud, but left with his terrified men. The haunting escalated over the next three years, with the spirit causing Betsy to break off an engagement to a young local named Joshua Gardner, and John Bell's health to decline. The spirit's shrill voice was heard by numerous witnesses, especially when it shrieked at 'Old Jack Bell'. John Bell finally died in 1820, and the spirit claimed that it had succeeded in poisoning him. In 1821 the spirit returned to Bell's widow, promising to pay another visit in seven years. It did reappear in 1828, at which point its interest seemed to centre on John Bell Jr. After a time, it swore that it would return in 107 years to haunt Bell's closest descendant. The mystery of the spirit was never solved; theories have ranged from a vengeful witch named Kate Batts who had been involved in a disputed financial transaction with Bell, to the ghost of a slave overseer, to a poltergeist caused by teenage Betsy, to fraud by the same girl – but the area around the Bell farm continues to be a locus of paranormal activity, especially a cave now known as the Bell Witch Cave.

Spirits in Europe were not confined to isolated farms, quaint ruins or Christianity. In the sixteenth century, the Jewish mystic Isaac Luria – now considered to be the father of contemporary Kabbalah – proposed the doctrine of transmigration of souls, or *gilgul*. As this idea spread throughout the Jewish population, so did belief in the *dibbuk* (or *dybbuk*), the spirit of a dead person that could gain possession of a living human who had secretly sinned. Luria's disciples gathered manuscripts detailing rituals for the exorcism of the *dibbuk*; the invading soul would then undergo transmigration or enter Hell.[11] In 1916 the Russian writer Shloyme Zanvl Rappaport – known by the pseudonym S. Ansky – wrote the play *The Dybbuk*, which brought the folklore of the invading spirit to worldwide attention (Rappaport died in 1920, tragically penniless, before the play was first produced). *The Dybbuk* is about Khonnon and Laia, whose fathers swore to see their children married to each other one day. After Khonnon dies, he returns as a *dibbuk* and takes possession of Laia; during her exorcism (which involves candles, scrolls and blowing the *shofar*, or ram's horn) the secret of the broken betrothal is revealed: Laia's father killed Khonnon to allow her to marry a rich man instead. During the exorcism, the *dibbuk* speaks through Laia, revealing his melancholy existence:

> I have no place to go. All roads are blocked for me, and all gates shut. Evil spirits surround me from all sides, waiting to devour me ... There is heaven and there is earth, and there are numberless worlds in the universe, but in not one of them can I find a resting place.[12]

*The Dybbuk* spawned several film adaptations, a television version directed by Sidney Lumet in 1960, operas and ballets.

The *dibbuk* was at the centre of a twenty-first-century paranormal happening now known as the Dybbuk Box. In 2003 a man named Kevin Mannis purchased a wine cabinet at an estate sale, and soon began to experience disturbing events, including breaking light bulbs, a hysterical employee and an intense smell of cat urine. When he presented the box to his mother as a gift on 31 October, she experienced a stroke the same day. Mannis tried to give the box away, but it was always returned to him with complaints ranging from nightmares to the cabinet's doors opening by themselves (one couple returned the box with a note that read 'This has a bad darkness').[13] Mannis sold the box on eBay, and other owners also claimed to experience uncomfortable incidents before selling the box. The last owner, Jason Haxton, eventually hid the box. The film *The Possession* (2012) is loosely based on the story of the Dibbuk Box.

Russian folk tales, or *skazkas*, collected around the turn of the twentieth century also paint a picture of returning spirits as malevolent and vengeful. W.R.S. Ralston describes ghosts that bear some resemblance to the Scandinavian *draugar*:

> It is not as an incorporeal being that the visit from the other world is represented in the Skazkas. He comes not as a mere phantom, intangible, impalpable, incapable of physical exertion, haunting the dwelling which once was his home, or the spot to which he is drawn by the memory of some unexpiated crime. It is as a vitalized corpse that he comes to trouble mankind, often subject to human appetites, constantly endowed with more than human strength and malignity.[14]

In a *skazka* called 'The Shroud', for example, a lazy girl persuades her friends to do her spinning chores for her, but on condition that she go to the church near the graveyard and take a certain picture. While passing the graveyard, the foolish girl spots a corpse in a shroud, and she takes the shroud. Not long after she arrives home, the corpse appears at her window, demanding the return of the shroud and telling the girl that she must return it where she took it – in the graveyard. The girl refuses to return to the cemetery, and the corpse appears again the next night, this time to the girl's parents. Once again, the girl refuses. The next day the parents entreat the help of the priest, who performs a special service in the church – which is interrupted when a strong wind roars through the church and the girl vanishes.

In 'The Two Corpses' the returned dead acts more like a modern zombie. A soldier is passing through a cemetery when he realizes that he is being chased by a corpse. He flees into a chapel, where another corpse is laid out for burial. The soldier hides in a corner, and the corpse that had chased him rushes into the chapel, waking the second corpse, who asks what he is doing. 'I've chased a soldier in here,' answers the first dead man, 'so I'm going to eat him!' The two corpses fight over who will eat the soldier until the cock's crow signals the arrival of dawn, at which point they both fall lifeless to the ground and the soldier escapes.

Another story, 'The Dog and the Corpse', also features an armed man (in this case, a hunter) being chased through a grave-yard, but this tale includes the more typically ghostly description that the corpse was 'not touching the earth with its feet, but keeping about a foot above it – with the shroud fluttering after it'.[15]

A new religion appeared in the nineteenth century, one with considerably more sympathetic views of spirits and the afterlife. In 1848 an English novelist named Catherine Crowe found her greatest success with a non-fiction book titled *The Night-side of Nature*; the book not only became arguably the most famous ghost book of the nineteenth century, but was also undoubtedly a major influence on the burgeoning Spiritualism movement. In the introduction to her book, Crowe discusses the transition from the credulity of the Dark Ages through the scepticism of the Restoration to the more metaphysical mindset of the nineteenth century:

> The contemptuous scepticism of the last age is yielding to a more humble spirit of enquiry; and there is a large class of persons amongst the most enlightened of the present, who are beginning to believe, that much which they had been taught to reject as fable, has been, in reality, ill-understood truth.[16]

Other books were also pointing the way to a new religion, one founded on a strong belief in ghosts. In the late eighteenth century the Swedish mystic Emanuel Swedenborg claimed that God had given him the ability to talk to a variety of unearthly spirits, and that he was determined to use his new gift to reform Christianity. In 1847 an American clairvoyant and faith healer, Andrew Jackson Davis, published *The Principles of Nature, Her Divine Revelations, and a Voice to Mankind*, which played a significant part in the development and spread of Spiritualism. Davis put forth the belief that 'man possesses a visible form, which serves as a medium through which he associates with things *invisible* and *eternal*', and he went on to discuss his beliefs in the use of 'magnetism' and 'electricity' by mediums.[17]

However, Spiritualism was really given its start by a remarkable series of events that occurred in a small American village – events that ignited a Western obsession with ghosts that would continue into the next century. In December 1847 the Fox family moved to the New York village of Hydesville. Within days of their arrival they began to notice strange things happening in their new home: loud rapping, furniture that seemingly repositioned itself, beds that rocked by themselves. Over the next three months, the phenomena continued to increase in both frequency and decibels. The Foxes' youngest daughter, Kate, soon discovered that the spirit would respond to questions and requests. When a neighbour suggested that the spirit could communicate by rapping at the appropriate points as letters of the alphabet were read aloud, Kate, her sister Margaret and their mother were happy to comply. The spirit named itself Charles Ryan, and gave as its reason for reaching out from beyond the grave the goal of proving once and for all that survival after death was possible.

The Foxes were soon in such demand as mediums that they moved their operations to Rochester, where they held public séances. Following the success of the Foxes, mediums sprang up all over the world, bringing the new metaphysics of 'Spiritualism' with them. Unfortunately for the Foxes, they were eventually exposed by a relative, Mrs Norman Culver, to whom they had confided their secret: 'The raps are produced by the toes. All the toes are used. After a week's practice with Catherine showing me how, I could produce them perfectly myself.'[18]

In 1877 estimates of the number of Spiritualists in the USA ran from two million to as high as eleven million. Spiritualists frequented séances, typically held in private living rooms, where they might be witness to levitation, teleportation of objects, ghostly music, apparitions, the production of ectoplasm and mediums released from various bonds by spirit assistants.

The Fox family home as it stood in Lily Dale, before it burned down.

Possibly the most popular of all the Spiritualist mediums were
William and Ira Davenport, two Americans whose father was a
police detective. Intrigued by stories of the Fox spirit rappings,
the Davenports decided to try their own spirit communication,
and started claiming 'John King' as their ethereal guide (although
in a pamphlet about the Davenports in 1864, the spirit was identified as 'Johnny King'; his real name was Sir Henry Morgan and
he had once been the Governor of Jamaica).[19] In 1855, when Ira
and William were (respectively) just sixteen and fourteen, they
began giving public performances in rented halls; their repertoire
quickly expanded beyond the usual table tipping and rapping to
include floating musical instruments and 'spirit hands' that tugged
at spectators. The Davenports next introduced the 'spirit cabinet'
into their act. This was a large enclosure within which they were
placed – usually bound by rope – and from which various phenomena apparently originated. The Davenports' real talent was their
escape magic, which would later be employed by a young magician
named Harry Houdini (who befriended Ira shortly before the latter
died in 1911). Although the Davenports never called themselves
'mediums', they nevertheless labelled their performances as séances,

The Davenport brothers, *c.* 1860.

and so invited the close scrutiny of such sceptics as the famous conjurer J. N. Maskelyne. Maskelyne studied their act until he could copy it exactly, and from 1883 to 1884 he gave 200 performances of his imitation séance at the Egyptian Hall in London.

In 1875 an attractive blonde named Annie Fay arrived in London, supposedly armed with a great talent for spirit communication. Fay's act consisted of inviting about twenty people to join her in a circle in a dark room; as the onlookers held hands, Fay began to clap hers. Although her clapping never broke off, the room began to echo with the sounds of musical instruments apparently played by spirit hands, and the sitters were touched in the darkness. Fay was even invited to the home of the distinguished British scientist William Crookes, an early pioneer of vacuum tubes, and after the medium was able to pass the tests to which Crookes subjected her, the scientist declared her powers genuine. Unfortunately, her fraudulent methods were soon exposed – including employing hidden assistants – but Fay continued to present her act until 1924. As Ira Davenport had done, Fay also confessed some of her secrets to Houdini.

New mediums appeared frequently throughout the Spiritualism craze, each finding fresh ways to present spirit communication. With 'spirit materialization', those participating in a séance could expect to witness a ghost; Spiritualists suggested that these materializations were effected when the ghosts were able to borrow 'atoms' from the participants for use in creating a visible form. Several other famed mediums produced 'slate-writing' as evidence, messages supposedly written on slates by spirits, sometimes in answer to a

A medium's assistant is caught in the act in this engraving, 1864.

sitter's questions. Both spirit materializations and slate-writing frequently involved hidden assistants, and both were exposed time and again.

As Spiritualism and the mediums at its centre continued to be exposed as frauds, the movement somehow gained strength. Proponents suggested that even those mediums who ended up showing exactly what tricks they used to achieve spirit communication had made a few authentic connections, although they also suggested that 'evil spirits' had occasionally tricked the tricksters into exposing themselves. In his book *Footfalls on the Boundary of Another World* (first published in 1859), Robert Dale Owen offers this possibility in the introduction to his collection of ghost narratives:

> If it may be plausibly argued that we cannot reasonably imagine spirits revisiting the scenes of their former existence with no higher aim, for no nobler purpose, than these narratives disclose, it must be conceded also, for the very same reason, that men were not likely to invent stories of such a character with no actual foundation whereupon to build. Imagination, once at work, would not restrict itself to knockings, and scrapings, and jerking furniture about, and teasing children, and similar petty annoyances. It would conjure up something more impressive and mysterious.[20]

Sceptics asked why spirits could not manifest in broad daylight, and why séances were not held in well-lit rooms. Orrin Abbott, the companion to and chronicler of the Davenport brothers, proposed that light was an 'agitated' condition in which spirits could not manifest:

> Physiological works show that our bodies are continually undergoing a change, new particles from our food being added, and particles which are growing old, taken from us and thrown off. The manifesting spirits claim that with the use of electricity, they collect particles thrown off from the mediums, and form bodies and limbs which they control with more

George
Cruikshank,
*Ghost of
Stockings*, 1864.

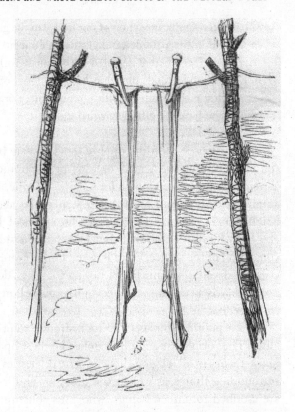

readiness than they formerly used their own tenements of clay.
But light, say they, makes it more difficult to collect and hold
those particles in compact bodies.[21]

Non-believers also asked why ghosts should appear clothed.
If a ghost was the spirit of a deceased person, why would it not
appear naked? Did its frock coat or leather boots somehow pass
on with it? In *A Discovery Concerning Ghosts*, George Cruikshank
even suggested that each article of clothing, be it a suit of armour
or a single undergarment, must have its own ghost. In response,
the medium and proponent of Spiritualism Newton Crosland
proposed this explanation:

That every significant action of our lives – in the garments we wear, and in the attitudes and gestures of our humanity – is vitally photographed or depicted in the spirit-world; and that the angels, under God's direction, have the power of exhibiting, as a living picture, any specific circumstances or features to those who have the gift of spiritual sight.[22]

Humorists of the time openly mocked true believers, as in the piece 'Among the Spirits' of 1861 by the immensely popular 'Artemus Ward' (a pseudonym for Charles Browne, a writer greatly admired by Abraham Lincoln). The writer talks about joining his neighbours in a séance, during which the spirits of 'Bill Shakspeer' and John Bunyan reveal that they have set up a sideshow. At the conclusion of the séance, Ward is asked for his opinion, and he decries the deceit of the mediums, noting that they 'don't do nobody no good & is a cuss to society & a pirit [pirate] on honest peple's corn beef barrils'.[23]

Many political thinkers also took strong exception to Spiritualism. The sociologist and philosopher Herbert Spencer created a ghost-theory of all religious beliefs: 'The properties and actions of surrounding things, as well as the thoughts and feelings of men, are ascribed to unseen beings, who thus constitute a combined mechanism of causation.'[24]

And, strangely, religious men also objected to Spiritualism. Even though the movement embraced Christianity, Catholic priests were uncomfortable with the idea of communicating with the dead. In his book *The Spirits of Darkness*, Reverend John Gmeiner offers up this strong criticism: 'Modern Spiritualism is substantially but a revival of ancient pagan practices, known already many centuries before Christ, and condemned as abominable by Moses.'[25]

Stories of wraiths or 'fetches' – the spirits of living persons who visit others at a time of death or trauma – remained popular throughout the nineteenth century. Some involved persons who were highly placed enough that they generated newspaper headlines and talk among Spiritualists of how they constituted proof of the existence of ghosts. One such case involved Sir Edmund Hornby,

Chief Judge of the Supreme Consular Court of China and Japan. In January 1875 Sir Edmund claimed that one night he was awakened at about 1 a.m. by a reporter who asked for the results of the day's court cases. Sir Edmund, anxious not to wake his wife, reluctantly complied and wrote out a short article, with which the reporter left. The next day Sir Edmund discovered that the reporter had died at about 1 a.m. from heart problems.

Not all the attention attracted by this case was positive. The editor of the *North China Herald*, a Mr Balfour, was well acquainted with both Sir Edmund and the late reporter, and noted that Sir Edmund's wife had, at that time, been dead two years; the case Sir Edmund mentioned in the article was non-existent; and the reporter had in fact died between 8 and 9 a.m. Mr Balfour concluded:

> It is probable that similar stories of the kind would collapse in a similar manner, were they tested properly by independent observation and inquiry, and were someone willing to take the trouble to make the inquiry and, having made it, to take the trouble of contradicting and exposing them.[26]

In 1884 Spiritualism was dealt a blow that did seem finally to diminish its popularity significantly. A gentleman named Henry Seybert died, and left a sum of money to the University of Pennsylvania for the establishment of a Chair of Philosophy, under the provision that the university appoint a commission to investigate Spiritualism. The commission began to question mediums, but found most of them reluctant to submit to any form of test; those who did were revealed as frauds. In concluding the 159-page report, which was published in 1887, the chairman of the Commission, Horace Howard Furness, noted that in his experience, 'Dante's motto must be inscribed over an investigation of Spiritualism, and all hope must be abandoned by those who enter it.' Yet Furness – probably aware of the money bequeathed to the university by an ardent Spiritualist – also stated that he 'cannot think it right to pass a verdict, universal in its application, when far less than the universe of Spiritualism has been observed'.[27]

As the twentieth century dawned, Spiritualism and belief in ghosts might have been expected to fade when placed against the new technological wonders of electric light, motor cars, telephones, motion pictures and so on, but the idea of life after death was, as Carl Jung noted, a 'primordial image' and not likely to be replaced by mere gadgets. Jung himself had a number of supernatural encounters that confirmed his own faith, including this one from 1916:

> Around five o'clock in the afternoon on Sunday the front doorbell began ringing frantically . . . but there was no one in sight. I was sitting near the doorbell, and not only heard it but saw it moving. We all simply stared at one another. The atmosphere was thick, believe me! Then I knew that some-thing had to happen. The whole house was filled as if there were a crowd present, crammed full of spirits.[28]

The great inventor Thomas Edison's belief in ghosts led him to attempt to create a machine that would facilitate communication with ghosts. And what of the century's other prominent scientific genius, Albert Einstein? When asked if he believed in ghosts, Einstein answered: 'When twelve other persons have witnessed the same phenomenon at the same time, then I might believe.'[29] However, Einstein's theories regarding the conservation of energy have been used by ghost-hunters to try to establish a scientific basis for the existence of ghosts. If all energy is constant, they argue, where does that energy go when we die? The fact is that the energy is distributed into the environment (as heat) and into other organisms that consume our remains, but believers continue to suggest that it is impossible to account thus for all the energy in a living body.

Einstein's theory seemed to support the work of a scientist named Dr Duncan MacDougall, who in 1907 studied dying patients and concluded that upon death we lose exactly 21 grams. Was 21 grams the weight of a human soul? Unfortunately, MacDougall's methodology was shoddy, and his results were so inconsistent that they were dismissed almost immediately.

On 28 July 1914 an event occurred to shake the foundations of humankind, including those that dealt with the human spirit: Archduke Franz Ferdinand of Austria was assassinated, triggering a war that would claim tens of thousands of lives and create devastation on a scale previously unknown. The First World War left grieving survivors all over the world who were willing to listen to anyone who promised contact with those they had lost in battle, and the popularity of Spiritualism was renewed. Among the best-known proponents of twentieth-century Spiritualism was Sir Arthur Conan Doyle, the creator of Sherlock Holmes. Doyle toured giving lectures on Spiritualism, and wrote books on the subject in which he discussed encounters with the 'whispering voices of the dead' and 'graceful lights' at séances.[30]

That the author behind one of literature's most supremely rational heroes could be deceived not just by fraudulent mediums but by the famous Cottingley Fairies photographs (which purported to show real fairies, but in reality were produced using cardboard cut-outs positioned before a camera by two young girls) mystified no one so much as Doyle's friend Harry Houdini. In the 1920s Houdini and Doyle had a close friendship that remains one of the most curious relationships in the history of ghost-hunting: Houdini, the genius magician and escape artist who exposed dozens of fraudulent mediums, saw Doyle as astonishingly credulous, while Doyle for his part believed that Houdini possessed genuine psychic abilities. Nonetheless, the two men respected each other's talents and shared a mutual interest in participating in psychic investigations; however, their friendship came to an abrupt halt when Doyle and his wife insisted on staging their own séance with the Houdinis, during which Mrs Doyle, acting as medium, claimed to speak with the voice of Houdini's mother.

One medium whom both Doyle and Houdini investigated in 1920 was the immensely popular 'Eva C.' The production of 'ectoplasm' had become a common event during séances; the ethereal material – described variously as gauzelike, rubbery and gelatinous – exuded from the medium's body. The French physiologist and Spiritualist Charles Richet was the first to use the word 'ectoplasm' to describe this material, in about 1900, but he believed it to be associated with non-ghost supernatural phenomena. Other Spiritualists, however, thought ectoplasm was the substance that enabled certain ghosts to become visible; after a medium produced the ectoplasm, which was invisible at first, spirits could don it like a cloak.

Eva Carrière (Eva C.) claimed to be able routinely to produce ectoplasm. Born Marthe Béraud, she had first held séances in 1905 in Algiers, where she claimed to produce the spirit of a 300-year-old Brahmin Hindu named Bien Boa. After the 'spirit' was revealed to be a local coachman, Béraud changed her name and began producing ectoplasm. Her performances were received enthusiastically, probably thanks in part to the fact that she often stripped naked for her audiences in an attempt to prove that she was hiding nothing. In 1920 Houdini attended a number of her séances, during which she produced examples of ectoplasm, including, as he reported, 'something that looked like a small face, say 4 inches in circumference'.[31] At the end of one séance, Eva produced ectoplasm from her mouth and then made it vanish – with a sleight-of-hand move that Houdini recognized. Houdini – who, despite his reputation as one of history's great debunkers, was willing to believe in anything that would put him in touch with his 'sainted mother' again – tried to approach séances with an open mind, but invariably left disappointed. In his book *A Magician Among the Spirits*, he noted of Eva C.: 'I was not in any way convinced by the demonstrations witnessed. I believe that Eva's feats are accomplished by regurgitation. If not, the work she is reputed to do is an "inside job".'[32]

It took another debunker to identify Eva C.'s 'ectoplasm' correctly. Harry Price had originally intended to pursue a career in archaeology, but became involved with researching psychic phenomena and mediums, and is now considered the greatest ghost-hunter of the twentieth century. Like Houdini, he was interested in magic and skilled at detecting fraud; in the case of Eva C., he pronounced her ectoplasmic faces to be nothing more than illustrations cut out of magazines (other researchers analysing her productions declared the ectoplasm to be no more than chewed paper). Price continued to investigate ectoplasm-producing mediums, who, he soon realized,

Harry Houdini (1874–1926) demonstrates how to make 'spirit hands' (presumably formed from ectoplasm) for use in séances.

were in the nasty habit of hiding the 'ectoplasm' in their vaginas until show time. In 1931, while investigating a medium named Helen Duncan, Price designed a special garment that would preclude her from using her hands or from producing anything from bodily orifices below the waist. Duncan, however, still managed to produce ectoplasm, at which Price realized that she possessed an extraordinary talent for regurgitation. When investigating a length of ectoplasm produced in 1939 by Duncan (and now kept in the library at Cambridge University), the writer Mary Roach opened a box containing a sheet of what was obviously cotton, roughly 3 m by 1 m (10 x 3 ft), which an accompanying note claimed had been extracted not via regurgitation but from Duncan's vagina.[33]

Price's renown as a ghost-hunter continued to rise, partly because of his skill at showmanship. On 10 March 1936 he led the first live radio broadcast of the investigation of a haunted house – Dean Manor, near Rochester in Kent – and his book of 1940 on his investigation into the haunting of Borley Rectory is a classic in the paranormal field, still reprinted to this day. Borley Rectory was built on the site of a monastery that had supposedly been home to a tragic love affair between a monk and a nun, an affair that ended with both dying (in one version, he kills her before being captured and beheaded; in another version, they are captured by his brother monks, who kill him and wall her up alive in the monastery). Servants working in the grounds of the rectory had reported hearing slipper-clad feet in hallways, glimpsing nuns in the surrounding wood and coming across late-night appearances of a phantom coach.

In 1929 Price was asked to investigate the rectory; not long after his arrival, he glimpsed a dark spectre in the woods and witnessed objects moving of their own accord. Among the oddest of the happenings at the rectory was a series of messages found written on the walls in pencil; the messages were directed to Marianne Foyster, whose husband had taken charge of the rectory in 1930. The messages were badly scrawled and usually illegible; the few words that could be made out seemed to indicate a speaker who was not accustomed to using English ('Marianne – Please help get'). Price saw the unreadable quality of these messages as proof that they were genuine ('practical jokers would not have been content to make mere lines, dots and half-formed letters on the walls').[34] After Price's death in 1948, there was considerable suggestion that he might have taken his innate showmanship too far and perpetrated an elaborate hoax at Borley. Although the rectory burned down in 1939 and was demolished in 1944, the site continues to provide ghost sightings. A photograph taken

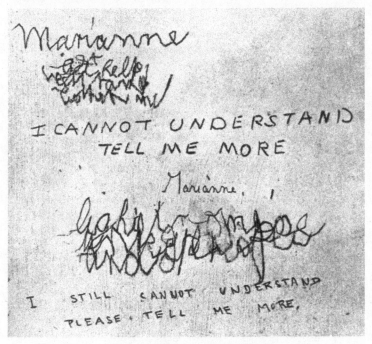

Spirit message found on the walls of Borley Rectory.

there in 1996 showed what looked like a ghostly monk in front of a contemporary building.

Mediums continued to collect headlines in the 1930s, although they were debunked with such increasing speed and frequency that Spiritualism finally began to ebb. Physical mediums – those who could produce physical manifestations such as table rapping or ectoplasm (as opposed to mental mediums, who merely reported messages and encounters with spirits) – made larger claims, such as the Welsh medium Colin Evans, who said that he was levitated by spirits during his séances. To prove his assertion, in 1937 Evans sent newspapers a photograph that purportedly showed him levitating during a performance; however, observers spotted a cable release in one of Evans's hands, making it apparent that he had simply jumped mid-séance (his sessions were conducted in the dark) and used the cable to trigger the flash photograph himself.

A TABLE LEVITATION.

This photograph shows the exact position of the hands and feet of the medium during one of our levitations. It will be observed how far they are removed from the table. [From a photograph specially taken to illustrate this manifestation.]

The medium Eusapia Palladino levitates a table, 1909.

Despite the evidence stacked against the mediums at its centre, Spiritualism refused to disappear completely, and it continues to this day as both an organized religious belief, with hundreds of churches in the USA and the UK, and an individual practice. The nineteenth-century British medium Emma Hardinge Britten is now considered to be 'the mother of modern Spiritualism'; she created the seven principles of modern Spiritualism (which include such items as 'Personal Responsibility' in addition to the 'Continuous Existence of the Human Soul'), and in the 1880s and '90s worked to unite the various Spiritualist churches found around the UK at the time.

If Spiritualism could be said to have its own Jerusalem, that would undoubtedly be a small town in New York called Lily Dale (the town's website proclaims it to be the 'World's Largest Center for the Religion of Spiritualism'). Founded in 1879 nearly 100 km (60 miles) south of Buffalo, Lily Dale (to which sceptics like to refer as 'Silly Dale' or 'Spooksville') has a summer season, during which it draws around 20,000 visitors who come to see its nearly 50 regis-tered mediums. The town once offered visitors the opportunity to tour the Fox Sisters' cottage, moved from Hydesville (it burned down in 1955), and now provides public demonstrations of mediumship (included with the small 'gate fee' charged to enter the town), workshops, ghost walks, forest hikes (some believe the surrounding forest to be inhabited by elementals) and shopping.

In about 1925 a new word began to appear in both psychology textbooks and ghost-hunting articles: parapsychology. Parapsychology was the study of paranormal phenomena using more scientific means, and it sprang from the work of the nineteenth-century psychic investigators. In 1882 the British physicist William Barrett and journalist Edmund Dawson Rogers founded the Society for Psychical Research (SPR), the first group dedicated to a more sober investigation of various supernatural phenomena. In 1886 the society produced *Phantasms of the Living* (written mainly by Edmund Gurney), a study of more than 700 cases of telepathy, hallucination and wraiths. Although the massive two-volume work specifically does not address 'apparitions of the dead', at about the time it was published, society members Richard Hodgson and S. J. Davey were demonstrating fraudulent techniques used by mediums by staging public fake séances. The society established a psychical research library, and in 1885 the American Society for Psychical Research was founded.

As Harry Price was busy debunking fraudulent mediums and investigating haunted places, others were exploring different areas in the new field of parapsychology. In the late 1930s a Hungarian psychologist living in Britain created a furore in Spiritualist circles by suggesting that there might be a psychological (and human) basis for many of the phenomena associated with ghosts. While working as a reporter in America in the early 1920s, Dr Nandor Fodor had become interested in psychic phenomena after reading Hereward Carrington's book *Modern Psychic Phenomena*. He began a friendship with Carrington, who was a writer and investigator, and started looking into strange cases himself. In his book *The Haunted Mind*, Fodor laid out his basic working principle: 'The paramount question for a psychical researcher is this: "Are the reported phenomena objective or not?"'[35] In 1936 he investigated a case known as the Ash Manor

Ghost, which created a stir in Spiritualist and parapsychological circles when Fodor's analysis of it came out. The case involved a gentleman to whom Fodor refers as Mr Keel, who had recently purchased an old house, Ash Manor. Not long after moving his wife and sixteen-year-old daughter, Pat, into the house, Mr Keel began to hear strange rapping; one night he fled to his wife's bedroom after encountering a spirit dressed in a green Elizabethan smock. Mrs Keel also encountered the ghostly visitor, and reported (as her husband had) that upon trying to seize the intruder, her hand had gone through it. Mr Keel feared financial ruin should he sell the house, so instead he called in psychic investigators, including Fodor. Fodor visited the house in the company of a medium, Eileen Garrett, who entered a trance state and spoke in the voice of her 'spirit control', Uvani; Uvani hinted at troubles within the Keel family. When Fodor pressed Mrs Keel about Uvani's suspicion, she confessed that her relationship with her daughter was strained and that her husband was homosexual. Fodor hypothesized that ghosts might be drawn to 'those who put themselves in an unguarded psychological position'.[36]

Fodor's theories did not sit well with Spiritualists, and over the next decade he turned away from parapsychology and chose instead to analyse paranormal events from a psychological perspective. In the 1940s he revolutionized parapsychology by publishing two articles about his study of classic poltergeist cases (including the Bell Witch).

The poltergeist seemed to be the natural successor to the ghost. The word comes from German, and literally translates as 'noisy ghost' or 'rumbling ghost'; it was first used in the English language in Catherine Crowe's *Night-side of Nature* in 1848. However, the word and the concept both have a long and interesting history in Germany, where the term is first encountered in the works of Martin Luther (alongside other terms, such as *Rumpelgeister* and *spuken*). In 1530 Luther compiled a list of 114 of what he believed to be the worst of the Catholic Church's abuses, and number five on the list – running considerably higher even than the celibacy of priests – was poltergeists; Luther believed that the Catholic Church used tales of poltergeists and other spirits to keep the faithful returning to Mass. He even offered advice to those who might be dealing directly with poltergeists:

> He will not harm you or attack God's word. Do not doubt, for in my opinion none of those poltergeists are sent by God to punish us; of their own accord and for their own sport they vainly try to frighten us because they have no power to harm men. If that spirit had the power to harm, he would not be such a noisy fellow, but would do his mischief even before you had the chance to discover who did it.[37]

Three centuries later at least one critic of Spiritualism found it odd that the ghosts attending séances acted more like Luther's poltergeists. In 1863 the *London Quarterly Review* noted that 'it seems a suspicious circumstance that the old-fashioned visible ghost has in these modern *séances* been almost entirely superseded by the *Poltergeist* or noisemaking spirit.'[38] The article went on to say that while modern science had come far in identifying optical illusions, little investigation had so far gone into the audio equivalent.

By the twentieth century, poltergeists had begun to be removed from the realm of the afterlife, after being studied extensively by members of the SPR and other experts in the supernormal. In a study in 1908, SPR member Frank Podmore suggested that poltergeist activity had a human agent:

> The person who is the centre of the disturbance, and in whose absence nothing takes place, is generally a child, boy or girl; more rarely a young servant maid . . . in one or two instances we have actually been present during the performance, and have detected trickery on the part of the children; in other cases trickery has been detected at the time by others; sometimes the child has subsequently confessed to trickery.[39]

In 1930 Carrington disagreed with the analysis that all poltergeist cases involved deceit and trickery, suggesting that there might be

The haunted Tower of London.

another reason they were frequently associated with young people. He believed that blossoming sexual energy in adolescents might be 'externalized beyond the limits of the body'.[40]

Carrington, however, went on to applaud Fodor's psychoanalytic take on poltergeists, and by the 1940s – thanks, perhaps, in part to Fodor's psychological laying of ghosts – society's attitudes to the spirit shifted again. With noisy, rapping spirits demystified, literature and cinema turned once again to the shimmering Gothic ghost, although the spirits were now romanticized: the films *The Ghost and Mrs Muir* (1947) and *A Portrait of Jennie* (1948) were typical of 1940s fare in which the ghost seemed to have been rendered safe by having nearly all its more frightening aspects removed. In 1945 on-screen ghosts were tamed with the arrival of Casper, whose first cartoon short, *The Friendly Ghost*, set up the iconic character as a child ghost who is more interested in befriending humans than frightening them. By the 1950s interest in ghosts seemed to have waned overall, as they seemed largely absent from both cinemas and newspapers; paranormal investigation turned mainly to flying saucers.

In the 1960s a new era of permissiveness in storytelling allowed filmmakers to uproot the psychosexual subtext of classic ghost books, resulting in such films as Jack Clayton's *The Innocents* and particularly Robert Wise's *The Haunting*. In a decade of upheaval, though, one of the more significant events in relation to the popularity of ghosts was the arrival of the Jet Age. Travel suddenly became fast, luxurious and relatively affordable, and the resulting explosion in tourism brought local ghost sightings to worldwide attention. On 12 February 1957 – exactly 403 years after her execution – the ghost of Lady Jane Grey was said to have been seen at night by a guard on duty at the Tower of London. The young Welsh guardsman was badly frightened, but when he reported the sighting it was dismissed as 'too commonplace to bother with'.[41] And yet now, nearly 60 years later, that encounter is one of many routinely reported to tourists visiting the Tower; it joins tales of a ghostly bear and a white lady in souvenir books and websites.

The Tower of London is the epitome of a destination for ghost tourism: it combines a bloody history (as a prison, torture chamber and execution ground) with a central location in a major metropolis; it looks old and even somewhat unnerving, with its bars and stonework; its surroundings are mostly level, making it easy to walk about; and it has been home to the sort of detailed tales that provide good, well-structured fodder for ghost stories.

Ghost tourism may be in the future of Poveglia, a small island near Venice, Italy, often called 'the most haunted island in the world'. Poveglia has a perfect history: before the twentieth century, the 7-hectare (17-acre) island served as a quarantine point for plague victims, a refuge against barbarian invasions and a fortified lookout.

In 1922 the existing buildings – some dating back to the twelfth century – were converted into a mental institution, and rumours circulated that the facility's director conducted cruel experiments on many of the inmates. According to legend, he was driven mad by ghosts and threw himself from one of the towers; the facility closed in 1936.[42] Poveglia's reputation as a haunted location grew, especially after it appeared on the television series *Ghost Adventures* in 2009; it is said to be haunted by 'Little Maria', a young plague victim, as well as by the evil director and dozens of his victims. The island's status as 'forbidden' – it is not open to tourists, although it can be visited via either official channels or clandestine boat hire – has only added to its mysterious appeal. In 2014 the cash-strapped Italian government placed it on the auction block, and it sold to an Italian businessman for just €513,000. However, a month after it sold the government deemed the winning bid too low. The businessman had planned a luxury resort, and a local conservation group has petitioned the government to be allowed to manage the island.[43] Whatever its fate, it seems likely that Poveglia's haunted history will somehow figure in its future use.

New Orleans is frequently referred to as 'America's most haunted city', with much of the attention centred on a beautiful three-storey house at 1140 Royal Street – the LaLaurie mansion. Briefly owned by the actor Nicolas Cage – who says he bought it because he frequently visited Disneyland's Haunted Mansion as a child, and purchasing the LaLaurie house gave him the chance to own 'the actual thing' – the elegant residence has all the requisites for a must-see for ghost tourists, and indeed it features in numerous local ghost tours and walks.[44] It was purchased in 1831 by Madame Delphine LaLaurie and her husband, Dr Louis LaLaurie, and in 1833 rumours of atrocity began to surface, after a young slave girl chased by Madame LaLaurie fell to her death. In April 1834 a fire broke out at the house, and firefighters made a spectacularly horrifying discovery: in the attic were chained slaves, many of whom had been mutilated by LaLaurie in what seemed to be bizarre surgical experiments. An angry mob stormed the house; although the LaLauries escaped, the spirits of those who died in agony at

The LaLaurie mansion in New Orleans, *c.* 1920.

THE WARRINGTON HOUSE (HAUNTED HOUSE). 1140 ROYAL STREET. NEW ORLEANS. LA.

Madame's hands did not. Over the years the house served as a school, a home for delinquents and an apartment building, and ghost sightings were constant. Although owners (including Cage) over the last few decades have reported no encounters, the house retains its reputation and is a major draw for tourists.

Ghost walks have become big business all over the UK and America, offering those hungry for paranormal experiences the opportunity to take leisurely night strolls directly past or through supposedly haunted places. The Original Ghost Walk of York claims to be 'the first exclusive Ghost Walk in the world' (its website notes only that it began some time before 1973), and is fairly

Ghost tourism in action: the Original Ghost Walk of York.

typical of ghost walks around the globe.[45] Lasting several hours and costing £5, the walk is led every night by an appropriately theatrical guide dressed in black who takes his large audience past the bloody Clifford's Tower, York's haunted jail and several churches.

Even relatively sunny, modern cities like Los Angeles now boast ghost tours (although, given the size of Los Angeles, the tours tend to be driven rather than walked). Southern California has a few ghost stories that stem from historical outrages – most notably in Los Angeles' large Griffith Park, which is said to be haunted by the ghost of Petranilla de Feliz, a Californio who was set to inherit the land from her elderly bachelor uncle, who was manipulated, legend has it, into leaving the tract instead to two lawyers – but most of those associated with Los Angeles are, predictably, related to Hollywood and the film industry. The 'Haunted Hollywood' bus

Southern
California's
haunted
Griffith Park.

tour, for example, will take guests to the historic Roosevelt Hotel
on Hollywood Boulevard, said to be haunted by the ghost of
Marilyn Monroe.

Ghost tourism received a major boost in the twenty-first century
with the introduction of reality television shows such as *Ghost
Hunters* (2004–). Ghost walks and ghost tours expanded to include
paranormal investigations, usually offered at additional cost. In the
case of the Stanley Hotel in Estes Park, Colorado – sometimes
referred to as 'the most haunted place in America'– it could almost
be said that ghost tours saved the venerable structure. Built in 1909
by F. O. Stanley, co-inventor of the Stanley Steamer car, the hotel
was originally intended as a health resort (Stanley suffered from
tuberculosis), but eventually became a regular resort. Because of its
isolated location high in the Rocky Mountains, it was difficult to

The Stanley Hotel in Colorado – 'a Disneyland for ghosts'
and birthplace of *The Shining*.

access, especially in winter, and year after year failed to turn a profit.
In 1973 a travelling novelist and his wife stumbled across the hotel
one winter night, and checked into Room 217. There the writer had
several strange encounters he could not explain. He was Stephen
King, and his visit to the Stanley inspired him to write one of
the most famous ghost stories in history, *The Shining* (1977). The
Stanley did not begin to turn a profit until 1996, when it began to
capitalize both on its own potential as a filming location (the 1994
film *Dumb and Dumber* and the television miniseries of *The Shining*
were both shot there) and on its reputation as a 'Disneyland for
ghosts'. It now boasts a variety of acclaimed ghost tours, during
which visitors may encounter the spirit of F. O. Stanley's wife,
Flora, on the upstairs balcony of the concert hall, or that of a home-
less runaway named Lucy who once squatted in the basement of
the same concert hall. If quizzed about why the Stanley is home to
so many active spirits, the hotel's guides offer speculation about the

bed of quartz on which the structure is built (the peculiar energy of quartz can supposedly be used by spirits and 'sensitives').

Another landmark event in ghost history occurred during the 1960s, when, for the first time, a university took serious interest in the study of the paranormal. In 1967 the University of California in Los Angeles (UCLA) opened a parapsychology lab under the direction of the clinical psychologist Dr Thelma Moss. During its eleven years in operation, the lab investigated hundreds of reports of ghosts and poltergeists, but two stood out. In the first, a Culver City housewife named Doris Bither reported poltergeist activity, but when Moss and her associates Kerry Gaynor and Dr Barry Taff arrived to investigate, she described considerably more than just flying crockery and rapping noises – she claimed to have been raped. In an attempt to escape the forces assaulting her, Bither moved house, but the unusual occurrences followed her. The UCLA team eventually lost touch with her, but did later discover that she had had a troubled past, with difficult family relationships and early experiments with séances and Ouija boards – in other words, Bither fit the classic profile of what Taff called a 'poltergeist agent'. Bither's story was adapted by the writer Frank De Felitta for his novel *The Entity* (1978), which was in turn made into a film in 1982, starring Barbara Hershey.

Perhaps the most spectacular case investigated by UCLA's Parapsychology Lab, however, involved a haunted mansion on Holly Mont Drive in the Hollywood hills. In 1976 Taff was working in the lab when a young man rushed in, badly frightened by a series of supernatural events he claimed to have just witnessed during a party at the Holly Mont house. The next night Taff and a colleague visited the house, and witnessed flying books, a disconnected doorbell ringing and bananas that appeared at Taff's feet after he mentioned being hungry. Taff later had the opportunity to occupy the house for some time, during which he witnessed a dark apparition and dozens of instances of supernormal phenomena. Later, a neighbour discovered a tunnel running from beneath his house to the Holly Mont house, which he believed had probably been used to transport liquor during Prohibition. In the tunnel, the neighbour discovered a makeshift headstone with the date 1922 and the name

Regina. Although the Parapsychology Lab was dissolved in 1978, Taff continued to investigate the house into the twenty-first century, and believes it to be a genuine haunting (as compared to poltergeist activity).

In the 1970s, while the UCLA Parapsychology Lab was investigating hauntings (along with other paranormal phenomena, such as extra-sensory perception and Kirlian photography), a group in Canada inaugurated a very different kind of experiment. In 1972 a Toronto mathematician, A.R.G. Owen, and the psychologist Dr Joel Whitton embarked on an attempt to create a ghost. They first created a fictional character whom they named Philip Aylesford; they crafted a history for Aylesford that included his life and suicide in seventeenth-century Britain, and they assembled a group who would try to contact Philip. Initial attempts failed, but when the environment was adjusted (lights dimmed, temperature dropped) to create a more traditional 'séance', the group began to experience rappings; they even filmed the table lifting at one point.

While the Toronto group seemed to enjoy calling up Aylesford (in the videos they gleefully sing songs to which they think he will respond), a haunting in 1975 would prove to be both less cheerful and more controversial, as well as possibly the single most famous haunting of the twentieth century. On 18 December 1975 George and Kathy Lutz moved into a large, elegant three-storey house in Amityville, New York, with their three young children. When they had been shown the house, they had been told that it had been the site of a notorious crime: a year earlier, 24-year-old Ronald DeFeo had murdered six members of his family. The Lutzes were more interested in the price of the house (just $80,000) and its large size, and they took it immediately. They spent 28 days in the house before fleeing with almost nothing. During those four weeks, they suffered what appeared to be a particularly Satanic haunting: crucifixes were hung upside down, hordes of flies appeared in the house (in the middle of winter) and a hidden 'red room' under the basement stairs inspired nightmares of animal sacrifice. A priest, Father Frank Mancuso, who was called into the house heard a deep voice behind him – in an empty room – command: 'Get out!'

The Lutzes found out that DeFeo's attorney had tried to argue that a force in the house had driven his client to commit the murders, and indeed, George Lutz began to experience hallucinations, hearing a marching band in the house and seeing his wife apparently change into a wizened hag. After the Lutzes abandoned the house, a group of psychics held a séance inside. The clairvoyant Lorraine Warren suggested that the presence in the house might be an elemental spirit: 'Whatever is here is, in my estimation, most definitely of a negative nature. It has nothing to do with anyone who once walked the earth in human form. It is right from the bowels of the earth.'[46] A documentary scriptwriter named Jay Anson wrote a book about the Lutzes' experience, and *The Amityville Horror* became a best-seller. In 1979 a film version starring James Brolin and Margot Kidder further sensationalized the account, adding walls of blood and a fly attack on the priest.

Although *The Amityville Horror* generated sequels in both film and book form, and a remake in 2005, it was eventually revealed that the entire haunting was a hoax, perpetrated by George Lutz (for financial reasons) and DeFeo's attorney, William Weber (seeking a new defence for his client). 'We created this horror story over many bottles of wine,' Weber told the Associated Press in 1995.[47] Later residents of the house confirmed that many of the details mentioned in the book could not be true (such as broken fixtures) and sued Anson, the Lutzes and the publishers for destroying their privacy by creating hordes not of diabolical flies, but rather of sightseers.

The extravagant action of the film version of *The Amityville Horror* was nothing compared to what was to come in the next decade. With improved special effects and a post-*Star Wars* emphasis on fast pace and high concept, films like *Poltergeist* (1982) and *Ghostbusters* (1984) took cinematic hauntings out of the realm of misty, frightening but powerless spirits, into one where deathless entities could kidnap children, destroy houses, open portals to other dimensions and finally transform into giant marshmallow men tramping through New York. Outside the cinema, the rise of haunted attractions likewise transformed the way the popular imagination thought of ghosts. Now anyone could experience a powerful spirit presence.

Over the last few decades, as belief in the paranormal has risen, ghosts have been involved in solving several crimes. Probably the most famous such case dates back to 1897, when the case of the Greenbrier Ghost fascinated Americans. After a young newlywed, Elva Zona Heaster Shue, was found dead in a log cabin in Greenbrier County, West Virginia, police failed to investigate, citing death by childbirth. Elva's mother, Mary Jane, was not satisfied,

The house from the 1979 film of *The Amityville Horror*.

however. For one thing, Elva had not been pregnant; for another, Mary Jane did not like her daughter's new husband, Edward. Mary Jane prayed for her daughter to come to her and reveal the truth, and over four successive nights that is exactly what happened. Elva detailed her death at Edward's hands, explaining how he had broken her neck. Mary Jane went to the police with this information and demanded an autopsy, which confirmed what the ghost had told her. Now a marker in the Greenbrier cemetery commemorates the Greenbrier Ghost, and calls it the 'only known case in which testimony from [a] ghost helped convict a murderer'.[48]

In 1978 Teresita Basa, a respiratory therapist working at the Edgewater Hospital in Chicago, was found murdered in her apartment. Basa, a native of the Philippines, had come to Chicago in the 1960s. The murder case was stalled until the investigating detectives received a strange call from police in nearby Evanston: they had been contacted by an elderly Filipino couple, the Chuas, who lived in a suburb of Evanston, and who had information on the case. The source of the information? The ghost of Teresita had supposedly taken possession of Mrs Chua one night, and, speaking through her, had named another hospital worker, Allan Showery, as the killer. Showery was interrogated and confessed, citing robbery as the motive.[49]

However, a ghost assisting in a murder trial in London in 1994 was not so helpful. A man named Stephen Young was found guilty of the double murder of the newlyweds Harry and Nicola Fuller, but a judge threw out the verdict after discovering that four of the jurors had made a Ouija board from letters and an upturned wine glass, and used it to contact Harry's spirit. The spirit had answered, and pointed out Young as the killer. Young's defence argued successfully that the use of the séance technique 'meant the jurors did not stick to the facts presented at the trial when deciding their verdict'.[50]

Now, in the twenty-first century, as a proliferation of ghost-hunting reality shows allow us all to be believers (if only for those few minutes between commercials), belief in ghosts is growing ever stronger. A poll in 2009 revealed that 65 per cent of Americans believe they have had a supernatural experience, 29 per cent had felt the presence of someone who had died and 18 per cent had been in the presence of a ghost. The last figure is especially notable for having doubled since 1996.[51] It seems that ghosts are in no danger of vanishing permanently.

# 4
# Hungry Ghosts: The Eastern World

Revere spirits, but keep them at a distance.
Chinese adage, attributed to Confucius

If ghosts in the Western world most often correspond to either our discomfort at being in abandoned structures or our desire to right old wrongs, it is interesting to ask whether ghosts from the other side of the world demonstrate the same relationships with people. In cultures where most of the major religions encompass reincarnation and the veneration of ancestors, we must enquire whether ghosts return for wholly different reasons, and whether they are as frightening and as popular in the arts.

The Chinese character for 'ghost' (*gui*, 鬼) is based on an early ideogram that depicts a human figure wearing a mask. Ghost masks in Chinese culture are traditionally fearsome, with fangs and bulging eyes, and the use of the mask suggests something disguised and unknown. The character for *gui* is at the root of many words for legendary monsters and creatures, indicating the importance of ghosts throughout Chinese culture. In the Chinese language, inflection is everything – the same word can have multiple meanings depending on minor changes in inflection – and one homonym for *gui* is the verb 'to return'. A popular Chinese belief is that each human has two souls, a 'mental soul', which ascends to Heaven at death, and a 'bodily soul', which remains on Earth and may become a ghost.

'Living under the ancestors' shadow is the central link between the Chinese world of human beings and their world of spirits', the anthropologist Francis Hsu has suggested.[1] If we begin our examination of Eastern ghost beliefs with China, then we should start

'The Ghost of Genji's Lover', a 19th-century illustration for
Lady Murasaki's classic *The Tale of Genji*, by Tsukioka Yoshitoshi.

with Taoism, the oldest of the three principal religions found there (the other two are Buddhism and Confucianism). Although Taoism is usually dated from Lao-tzu's classic work *Tao Te Ching* in the sixth century BCE, it incorporates many earlier practices, including the shamanism that was part of the early folk religions. Shamans were commonly employed to communicate and mediate with spirits, who were usually those who had not received a proper burial or been honoured by their descendants. In one classic account of early shamanism and ghosts, Prince Shên-Shêng of Chin was murdered by his father in 655 BCE. After five years of power struggles, Shên-Shêng's brother claimed the throne, and one of his first acts was to have Shên-Shêng disinterred and reburied without proper rites. Shên-Shêng's ghost soon visited one of his former retainers, and told him that God had decreed that, as a punishment for his brother's disrespect, the entire kingdom of Chin would be conquered by another country to the west. When the retainer mentioned that this punishment seemed unfair to all the innocents in Chin, the ghost agreed and instructed the retainer to seek out a particular shaman in seven days, while he returned to discuss this with God. In seven days the retainer met the shaman; Shên-Shêng's ghost spoke through the shaman and assured the retainer that punishment would be meted out only to the duke.

A description of two shaman sisters from the fourth century CE bears some resemblance to nineteenth-century Spiritualist mediums, who were also often female. The sisters were beautiful, performed a variety of tricks, such as spitting fire from their mouths, and produced 'spirit conversations [and] ghostly laughter'.[2]

Not all the early Chinese were believers. Ruan Zhan (281–310) was a sceptic whose arguments against the existence of ghosts (what came to be known as the 'no-ghost theory') were still being referred to 1,500 years later.

However, belief in ghosts and shamans extended all the way up the social ladder to the emperor, whose special shamans were known as *fang-shih* ('gentlemen with recipes'); their skills included communicating with and exorcising ghosts. An account of the court of Emperor Wu from the first century CE describes a Taoist *fang-shih* invoking the spirit of a favourite concubine, recently deceased: 'He set up candles and draped tents at night, laid out meat and wine, and had the Emperor sit in a separate tent. The Emperor saw a fine female figure in the distance just like Lady Li, who sat behind the drapery.'[3] Note the similarities to accounts of mediums from nineteenth-century Britain, using shadows and suggestion to produce 'spirits'.

In contemporary China, Taoist priests are thought to possess these same abilities. The priests are also able to help the deceased journey through Hell by preparing documents that the dead soul presents to the infernal magistrates, in the hope of easing the suffering that sinners must endure before they are allowed to reincarnate. 'Ghost money' – false notes in large denominations – is burned, since it is believed that the spirits in Hell will receive this money and may use it to advance or comfort themselves.

All the major Chinese religions celebrate the Hungry Ghost Festival (*Yü-lan-p'en,* or *Yu Lan*) on the fifteenth day of the seventh lunar month. It is believed that during this month the gates of Hell are opened and ghosts return to our world to commune with their families; those without families may become malevolent, and so food and entertainment are also provided for them, while smoke helps to drive them away. At the conclusion of the festival, the spirits are exhorted to return to their realm.

The Hungry Ghost Festival is one of the most important days in the Chinese calendar; like the Western Halloween, it also serves to mark the harvest and the changing of the season. The festival celebrates the opening of the gates of the underworld, when ghosts are released to return to their homes; it has been a popular celebration for nearly 2,000 years, and has inspired many stories, poems and songs. One of the most popular is a Tang Dynasty work known as 'The Transformation Text on Mu-lien Saving his Mother from the Dark Regions'. Mu-lien is a Buddhist adept with highly developed supernatural powers, who decides to find out how his parents are faring in the afterlife. He finds his father living happily in Heaven, but unfortunately a long search for his mother finally reveals her to be in the lowest depth of Hell, where Mu-lien finds her nailed down with 49 spikes. The Buddha intervenes and releases the denizens of Hell, but Mu-lien's mother is reborn as a hungry ghost who can never be satiated because food bursts into flames as it reaches her mouth. The Buddha appears again, this time instructing Mu-lien on how to prepare food for his mother on the fifteenth day of the seventh month. Mu-lien does as instructed, and his mother's ghost is finally released to Heaven.

Other stories surrounding Mu-lien detail his power of seeing these grotesque creatures when other mortals could not. Hungry ghosts (or *pretas*) were the spirits of those who had performed evil deeds in life and were condemned to wander as ghosts instead of moving on to a new life or to Heaven. A description is not likely to make anyone envy Mu-lien's ability to see them:

> *Pretas* are horrid monsters . . . They have long bristly hairs, arms and legs like skeletons. Their voluminous bellies can never be filled, because their mouths are as narrow as a needle's eye. Hence they are always tormented by furious hunger. Their colour, blue, black or yellow, is rendered more hideous still by filth and dirt. They are also eternally vexed by unquenchable thirst. No more but once in a hundred thousand years do they hear the word water, but when at last they find it, it immediately becomes urine and mud. Some devour fire and tear the flesh from dead bodies or from their own limbs; but they are unable to swallow the slightest bit of it because of the narrowness of their mouths.[4]

A number of the hungry ghost stories surrounding Mu-lien involve him discovering a *preta*; in such instances he finds the Buddha and asks what the ghost did in a previous life. The response is typically that the transgressor was the wife (or sometimes servant) of a wealthy landowner who offered to entertain a monk; however, the husband left, and the wife either tried to trick the monk or was simply cruel to him.

Another Mu-lien tale describes the origin of the Hungry Ghost Festival. One day the monk finds 500 hungry ghosts begging him to intervene on their behalf with their families to provide food for them. Mu-lien speaks to the families, who set up the feasts, but the monk is unable to find the hungry ghosts again. Puzzled, he seeks out the Buddha, who tells him that the ghosts are 'blown about by the wind of karma'. The Buddha agrees to bring the ghosts to the feast, and says their sins will be expunged as a result. The ghosts attain rebirth in Heaven, but descend again to honour the Buddha and Mu-lien.[5]

Mu-lien is not the only character in Chinese folklore who deals with ghosts. The figure of the ghost-hunter Zhong Kui emerged during the Tang Dynasty. Zhong was originally said to have been a physician who excelled in the imperial examinations, but when he attempted to save Emperor Xuanzong from a thieving demon, the emperor was repelled by his ugliness and refused to enrol him. Angered and shamed, Zhong Kui threw himself down the palace steps and died. The emperor immediately regretted his decision and ordered that Zhong Kui be buried with the highest honours. In gratitude, Zhong Kui returned as a ghostly ghost-hunter. His fearsome image, red-skinned and bushy-bearded, is displayed in many houses (especially around Chinese New Year) to keep ghosts

Ghost money is burned for ancestors to use in Hell.

Shōki the demon queller (Zhong Kui in Chinese) wearing the robes of a Chinese scholar. He is holding a sword in one hand and a demon in the other.

at bay. Zhong Kui is a beloved character in Peking opera, and also appears in Japanese culture under the name Shōki.

In some modern Chinese communities, especially Taiwan, the entire seventh month is celebrated as Hungry Ghost Month, and joss sticks are burned and food offered throughout the month. The festival is often celebrated with operas praising the gods, performed on temporary bamboo stages, and it has also become a tourist attraction. A Hong Kong tourism website notes: 'For the visitor, it's a perfect opportunity to see some of the city's living culture in action, with many people tending roadside fires and burning faux money and other offerings for ghosts and ancestors to use in the afterlife.'[6]

The Chinese have always had a fine tradition of *zhiguai* – 'strange stories' – the best-known collection of which is undoubtedly Pu Songling's *Strange Stories from a Chinese Studio* (1766, published half a century after Pu's death). Some historians believe that Pu found inspiration by setting up a stall on a busy thoroughfare and offering free tea to passers-by in exchange for stories of their more unusual experiences, so the tales collected in *Chinese Studio* can be considered representative of folklore at the time.[7] The tales in Pu's classic cover fox spirits (common in Chinese lore), gods, imps, doppelgängers and the spells of Taoist priests, but ghosts are also found in abundance. In fact, the first story in the book, 'Examination for the Post of Guardian Angel', is a ghost tale that demonstrates several of the essential differences between the Chinese and European approaches to ghosts. A recent graduate, Mr Sung, receives a call to an examination, which he passes in exemplary fashion. When told that he has been assigned to the post of Guardian Angel in another city, Mr Sung begs to be allowed to care for his 70-year-old mother before accepting the post. The ministers consult the Book of Fate and discover that Mr Sung's mother has nine years left to live; with that, they release Mr Sung to care for her. He awakens in his coffin, and his overjoyed mother tells him he's been dead for three days. He looks after her until her death, at which point he dies as well. His wife, who lives some distance away, witnesses him arrive suddenly in the hall, make an obeisance and depart. She later finds out that he was already dead. Another story in *Chinese Studio*, 'The Marriage of the Fox's Daughter', offers a trope that is immediately recognizable to readers around the world: a young man is challenged to spend the night in a haunted house. Rather than fearsome ghosts, he encounters a happy family of fox spirits celebrating a marriage.

'Judge Lu', meanwhile, describes a surprisingly gruesome world of ghosts and gods. The hero, Chu, is a brave, strong young man, but not particularly intelligent. One night he accepts a dare from drunken friends and breaks into a local temple, from where he steals the wooden statue of Judge Lu of Purgatory. His shocked friends beg him to return the statue, but before he does, he invites the judge to join him for a drink. The next night the judge appears at Chu's house, and although Chu is initially terrified, he soon realizes the judge has simply taken him up on his invitation. They become good friends, although the judge enjoys well-written essays and is disappointed by Chu's poor writing skills. One night Chu awakens with a pain in his abdomen, and finds the judge standing over him, having slit him open. He assures the horrified Chu that he is giving him a heart more suited to fine writing. Chu's new heart allows him to become successful, and he asks Judge Lu if his ugly wife could be made more beautiful. The judge appears soon thereafter with the severed head of a lovely young girl; he cuts off the head of Chu's wife and replaces it with that of the girl. Many years pass, and finally the judge comes to his friend and tells Chu that he will die in five days. Chu begs for more time, but Judge Lu tells him that 'to an intelligent man, life and death are much the same. Why necessarily regard life as a boon and death as a misfortune?'[8] Chu dies, but returns to care for his wife and son. He and the judge continue to drink at Chu's house, until his son reaches adulthood and Chu appears one night to bid his wife farewell for ever. When she questions him tearfully, he tells her that he has accepted a far-off post in the underworld.

*Strange Stories from a Chinese Studio* has remained popular for 250 years, spawning imitators, studies and film adaptations. In 2003 a new adaptation fell foul of the Chinese government because of the ghostly subject-matter, and many expected it to be banned. The ban was adroitly avoided, however, when the central ghost in the story was replaced by a Taoist Immortal.

Belief in ghosts continues to run through much of the Chinese population, and many cities in China have embraced ghost tourism. In Beijing, for example, visitors can stroll down Guije (Ghost Street), a lovely row of restaurants that was once lined with coffin shops and is now thought to be home to many ghosts; or visit the tomb of General Yuan, a loyal supporter of the Ming Dynasty, who was falsely accused of treason and put to death by the emperor. The locals were said to be so angry that they ate his remains, leaving only the head, which was saved by a loyal soldier. His ghost now wanders the area.[9]

Few places on Earth can claim as many gruesome and bizarre hauntings as Hong Kong. It is already a superstitious city – many buildings do not have a fourth floor because the Cantonese word for the number – *sei* – is a homonym for the word for death. In a city where living space is at a premium, apartments in which murders have taken place can be had for half the normal price, and in 2014 unnatural deaths occurred in an estimated 190 homes or apartments.[10] Several of Hong Kong's most haunted buildings derive their reputation from Japanese occupation and atrocities committed during the Second World War. The Sai Ying Pun Community Complex – known locally as the 'High Street haunted house' – was built in 1892 as quarters for European nurses, but was turned into an execution hall by the Japanese during the war, and became a lunatic asylum afterwards. The second floor is now said to be haunted by a diabolical figure dressed in traditional robes, who occasionally bursts into flames. However, nowhere in Hong Kong is more infamous than Nam Koo Terrace, which has reportedly 'been the scene of too many suicides, rapes and murders for authorities to keep count'.[11] Like that of the High Street haunted house, the history of Nam Koo Terrace is rooted in Japanese wartime occupation: it served as a brothel, where local women were raped and tortured. The headless spirits of the former victims are now said to haunt the building, spewing green smoke. Nam Koo Terrace made headlines in 2003 when a group of teenagers fled the house, including one girl who claimed to be possessed and required hospitalization.

As entwined as ghosts are in so many aspects of Chinese culture, they may be an even more crucial part of life in Japan:

> Death is not only a common subject in Japanese folklore but seems indeed to be the *principal* topic in Japanese tradition; nearly every festival, every ritual, every custom is bound up in some way with relationships between the living and the dead, between the present family and its ancestors, between the present occupation and its forebears.[12]

The Japanese follow Buddhist tradition in believing that a spirit takes 49 days (the sacred number seven, squared) to cross over to *anoyo*, the other world; during that time, the ghost may seek to atone for its sins or wreak vengeance. On the 49th day after a person's death, the *Shijū-kunichi*, or final funeral rite, is observed; at that point the ghost will have withstood ten trials in the afterlife, and its final destination (chosen from one of six different worlds) will be revealed. During the time leading up to *Shijū-kunichi*, the ghost will stay near its home, and one ritual (now largely obsolete) involved family members calling the dead loved one's name to help them return should they wander. The concept of *on* – the obligation to repay debts of both money and kindness – affects both the bereaved, who will put out food and read sutras for the departed, and the new ghost. Even a ghost who led a good life risks being consigned to Hell if the proper sutras have not been read in his or her name.

The Japanese celebrate the Hungry Ghost Festival as *Obon* or simply *Bon*. It takes place over several days, and begins with the lighting of a fire or candle in the garden or doorway, so that the wandering spirits can find their way home. The *Bon-odori*, a ritual dance, may be performed. The ancestors' tablets are set out on the family altar, along with offerings. *Obon* ends when small lanterns are released on a river or outgoing tide, since the visiting ghosts are believed to float away with them.

A hungry ghost in Japan is known as a *gaki*, while ghosts in general are *yūrei* (not to be confused with *yokai*, which are non-human supernatural spirits). There are many different types of *yūrei*, including *funayūrei*, ghosts of those who died at sea; *ubume*, mother ghosts who return to care for their living children; and *onryō*, vengeful ghosts.

In the seventeeth century, the Japanese not only had as many ghost stories as the Chinese, but even had a game dedicated to sharing them: *Hyakumonogatari Kaidankai* involved slowly extinguishing lights as participants told 100 ghost stories. This was thought to be a method for summoning spirits, so many players lost courage and left the game before the hundredth story was told.

A typical ghost story from this period might involve a *yūrei* like Yuki Onna, 'Snow Woman', who was thought to be a woman with white skin and a white kimono, usually seen in a snowy landscape. In some tales, Yuki Onna is the ghost of a woman seeking revenge; in others, she is a vampire wandering icy forests seeking victims; in a version recorded by Lafcadio Hearn (of whom more below), she kills an old woodcutter one night by sucking out his life essence, then promises to leave his son alive only as long as he never tells anyone what he saw. Some time later, a beautiful woman appears to the son; they fall in love, marry, have children and live happily. One

Lafcadio Hearn and his wife.

night the son tells her the story of Yuki Onna, at which his wife reveals herself to be the same. Disappointed that her husband has failed to keep his promise, she vanishes for ever.

One Westerner was responsible probably more than any other for first bringing Asian ghost stories to the English-speaking world:

Lafcadio Hearn (1850–1904). Hearn's father was Irish and his mother Greek, and as a child he had lived in both Greece and Ireland. When he was nineteen his family sent him off to Cincinnati in Ohio, where he found a job as a newspaper reporter. In 1890 his work took him to Japan, where he married, obtained citizenship and became a Buddhist. He collected and translated stories from old books and local residents, and his books, including *In Ghostly Japan* (1899), introduced many American and British readers to Japanese and Chinese lore. This passage from the opening of his most famous collection, *Kwaidan: Stories and Studies of Strange Things* (1903), makes the continuing interest in Hearn's works and Chinese/Japanese ghost stories clear:

> More than seven hundred years ago, at Dan-no-ura, in the Straits of Shimonoseki, was fought the last battle of the long contest between the Heike, or Taira clan, and the Genji, or Minamoto clan. There the Heike perished utterly, with their women and children, and their infant emperor likewise – now remembered as Antoku Tenno. And that sea and shore have been haunted for seven hundred years … Elsewhere I told you about the strange crabs found there, called Heike crabs, which have human faces on their backs, and are said to be the spirits of Heike warriors. But there are many strange things to be seen and heard along that coast. On dark nights thousands of ghostly fires hover about the beach, or flit above the waves – pale lights which the fishermen call Oni-bi, or demon-fires; and, whenever the winds are up, a sound of great shouting comes from that sea, like a clamour of battle.[13]

A contemporary Japanese urban legend combines both aspects of *Oboni* and the classic 'vanishing hitchhiker' ghost story. A taxi driver picks up a young woman in front of a hospital in Tokyo. She gives him directions, but when they arrive at her destination the cabbie finds that she has vanished, leaving behind only a cold seat. He speaks to someone inside the house she indicated, and they tell her that the woman died in hospital the day before.

No haunted place in Japan is more famous than Aokigahara, commonly known as 'Suicide Forest'. About 100 people die in the forest each year, many from drug overdoses or (most popularly) hanging. Legend has it that, in the distant past, tribes left their infirm elderly in the forest to die, and that their spirits now haunt it. Aokigahara has become such a popular place for suicides that the government has posted signs throughout it suggesting that those who have come to the forest for that purpose seek help. Aokigahara is said to have both a strange absence of wildlife and magnetic anomalies that render compasses useless, and there are reports of negative energy surrounding the place: 'Some survivors of suicide attempts in Aokigahara have told of having had the vague feeling of being somehow called to or pulled towards the forest, and of having the inexplicable compulsion to make the journey there.'[14]

Those who practise Northern Buddhism, as outlined in the *Bardo Thodol* (*Tibetan Book of the Dead*), believe in a cycle of reincarnation, which includes the notion that 49 days pass between death and the next rebirth. Three and a half days after death, the spirit receives visions of its destiny, one of which might concern rebirth as a *preta*; however, the fate shown in the visions can be avoided if the *bardo*-body follows the teachings given by the guru in the previous life. The spirit's karma will determine whether he or she experiences bliss or terror during this intermediate time, although confusion and desire for a body are normal:

> Thou wilt see thine own home, the attendants, relatives, and the corpse, and think, 'Now I am dead! What shall I do?' and being oppressed with intense sorrow, the thought will occur to thee, 'O what would I not give to possess a body!' And so thinking, thou wilt be wandering hither and thither seeking a body.[15]

*The Tibetan Book of the Dead* also states that feeling anger at one's successors or attachment to material goods during the moment of judgment may lead to rebirth as a *preta*. A ghost resides in the *bardo*-world for an indeterminate time, its evolution held back, before it moves on. These spirits may be called forth by *lamas* (high priests),

An *onryō*, or
vengeful ghost,
carries off a
man's severed
head in this
19th-century
hanging scroll
by Kawanabe
Kyosai.

and Buddhist teachings caution that none but the most advanced should attempt this sort of communication.

In India, Hinduism is the predominant religion, and equates ghosts with a belief in the 'second body', also known as the 'subtle body', which eventually moves on to reincarnate in a new corporeal form; these beliefs explain cremation – which prevents a ghost from re-entering its 'gross body' – as the preferred funeral practice in this religion. During the country's time as a British colony, Indian ghost stories often blended Eastern and Western traditions, and Indian literature under the Raj might find reincarnation combined with stories of haunted houses and spectral photography.

In India, belief in the *bhūta* or *bhoot* is still strong. This unhappy ghost may be formed by violent death or by the failure to observe proper burial rituals, and can be very troublesome to mortals. A *baiga* is a kind of 'cunning man' who specializes in dealing with ghosts and healing those who have been afflicted by ghosts or *bhuts*. A *baiga* might create charms from barley and recommend the sacrifice of an animal, but he always has a ready answer should his charms fail:

> If his patient die, he gets out of the difficulty by saying – 'Such and such a powerful Bhut carried him off. What can a poor man, such as I am, do?' If a tiger or a bear kills a man, the Baiga tells his friends that such and such a Bhut was offended because no attention was paid to him, and in revenge entered into the animal which killed the deceased, the obvious moral being that in future more regular offerings should be made through the Baiga.[16]

*Bhuts* have some intriguing characteristics: they are always hungry and thirsty; they avoid salt; they attack people who have just eaten sweets (which explains why sellers of sweets sometimes provide salt); they especially like milk; they may be very malignant if the spouse they left behind remarries; they may enter the body during a yawn and be expelled by a sneeze; and they cannot sit on the ground (because the Earth, as a goddess, frightens all evil influences). *Bhuts* always appear stark naked (thus answering one of the principal objections that nineteenth-century Western sceptics had to their ghosts, which were always described as clothed), and they sometimes abduct women. *Bhuts* can appear almost indistinguishable from human beings, but there are three tests for detecting a *bhut*: it will cast no shadow; it cannot endure the smell of burning turmeric; and it always speaks with a nasal twang.

A particularly malignant form of *bhut* is the *gayâl*, which is the ghost of a man who died without having children and thus has no one to perform customary after-death rites for him. Villages in India keep small platforms with bowl-like depressions into which milk and water are poured to conciliate the *gayâl*.

The *preta* is also found in India, although there the term may be applied to the spirit of a deformed person or a child who dies in premature birth. The *preta* are believed to be no bigger than a man's thumb, and the Indian *preta* are generally thought to be far less dangerous than the *bhuts*.

Among the most destructive and feared of Indian supernatural creatures is the *râkshasa*, which 'goes about at night, haunts cemeteries, disturbs sacrifices and devout men, animates dead bodies, even devouring human beings . . . He is emphatically a devourer of human flesh, and eats carrion.'[17] *Râkshasas* fly by night, fight with the gods and cause vomiting when they come near human beings. Some Hindus believe that the ghost of a Musalmân (Muslim) or Brâhman may become a most malignant *râkshasa*.

In 1993 an anthropological study of ghosts in a village in northern India offered some suggestions as to why belief in ghosts not only remains strong in this region, but also intensifies during especially stressful times:

> The fear of death and anxiety about becoming a ghost persist among villagers and are reinforced by a long history of many deaths, a relatively short life expectancy through centuries, and an ideological perspective about life and death deriving from Hindu beliefs about the soul (atman), the soul's actions (karma), and ghosts causing death.[18]

This study (which was actually conducted in the 1970s) found a wide range of ghost beliefs among the inhabitants of one village (Shanti Nagar), including atheism and even some Buddhists who did not believe in ghosts. However, certain beliefs ran through most of the village's population: a deceased person would become a ghost thirteen days after death; ghosts caused illness; the mentally ill suffered from possession by ghosts; and someone could become a ghost if they died before their intended time. The residents of Shanti Nagar named particular local ghosts whom they believed had caused illness and misfortune in the village. One, for example, 'the Headless Sweeper', was a man who had committed suicide when he was infected by plague (he cut off his own head with a knife). Because he died from 'deliberate death' but was also a plague victim, he was doubly cursed to return as a malevolent ghost.[19]

Throughout Asia, women who have died in childbirth are accorded special status in ghost lore. In Japan, the *ubume* might appear with a crying child in her arms; if followed, the *ubume* will vanish, but the child might be found alive, nestled in a grave. In northern India, Bangladesh and Pakistan, the *churel* is especially likely to result from a pregnant woman dying during Diwali, the Hindu festival of lights, and she will suck the blood of any male relatives who treated her poorly. The *churel* is sometimes linked to local goddesses – Porû Mâi of Nadiya, for example, is a mother goddess of the jungle who is also linked to a *baghaut*, the ghost of a man who was killed by a tiger. Perhaps most terrifying, though, is the Singaporean and Malaysian *pontianak*, which is said to haunt isolated roads, begging a lift from any men who might be driving alone. The *pontianak* will originally appear as a lovely, seductive woman, but – if the man should give in to the illusion – will suddenly manifest in her true, frightening form and slay the unwary driver. A *pontianak* leaves behind it the scent of frangipani, a flower usually associated with graveyards, and can be laid to rest by driving a metal spike through the back of its neck. The *pontianak* is so popular that it has inspired films, songs and even television commercials.

Contrast this with a belief from Polynesian mythology regarding ghost infants:

*Bhūta* sculpture at a Sarbojanin Kali Puja
Pandal at College Square, Kolkata.

If a child was born before its time, and thus perished without having known the joys and pleasures of life, it was carefully buried with peculiar incantations and ceremonies; because if cast into the water, or carelessly thrown aside, it became a malicious being or spirit, actuated by a peculiar antipathy to the human race, who it spitefully persecuted, from having been itself deprived of happiness which they enjoyed.[20]

## 5

# *La Llorona* and Dreamtime: Ghosts in Latin America and the Southern Hemisphere

Although the Chinese Hungry Ghost Festival is probably the world's most widely practised annual celebration of the spirits of the deceased, one other festival might rival it in terms of colourful imagery and fascinating history: Mexico's *Dias de los Muertos*, or Days of the Dead.

*Dias de los Muertos* – which, like *yü-lan-p'en*, can vary in length depending on the region – is a combination of indigenous Meso-american festivals and the Catholic observances of All Saints' Day (1 November) and All Souls' Day (2 November). On the far side of the world, when Catholic missionaries arrived in Celtic Ireland, they likewise co-opted the Celts' celebration of Samhain on 31 October for All Saints' and All Souls' days (or eves, since the Celts began each new day at sundown), and the result was Halloween. What little we know of Samhain suggests that it was a time of feasting with some playfully macabre aspects – it was the Celts' New Year, a time when they believed the veil between our world and the other world was thinnest. Some of that is certainly reflected in the modern celebration of Halloween.

*Dias de los Muertos*, however, incorporated existing celebrations that honoured the dead, mainly the Aztecs' *Miccailhuitontli* (Little Feast of the Dead) and *Miccailhuitl* (Great Feast of the Dead). The former honoured the spirits of deceased children, while the latter venerated adults.

*Miccailhuitl* began on 3 August. Food and drink were placed on the tombs of the dead for four years after their death, since the

*Dias de los Muertos* offering (or *ofrenda*).

Aztecs believed the soul had to endure a difficult four-year journey to the underworld of *Mictlan*. However, other accounts record the larger feast beginning on 23 August, and including a verbal invitation to the dead to join their families.

The Aztecs had a number of festivals dedicated to the dead, including separate celebrations of their deceased warriors and women who had died in childbirth. The Aztecs deified both these classes, and believed their souls went to separate worlds in the after-life (as did the spirits of infants who had died before eating solid food). However, the Spanish missionary Fr Bernardino de Sahagún (1499–1590) – whose enormous collection of Aztec history and

Day of the Dead sugar skulls, made from *alfeñique*
and decorated with frosting and glitter.

lore, *General History of the Things of New Spain* (also known as the
*The Florentine Codex*), remains our best record of Aztec beliefs –
did note that the Aztecs believed in ghosts.

There can be no question that the modern Days of the Dead
are really all about the spirits, however. Although the rituals and
even the number of days set aside for the festival vary from region
to region, the commonality is the belief that deceased family members return during this time, and must be honoured with offerings
of food and drink. Most areas begin the festival with a celebration
for children; the next night, the adult spirits are honoured. *Ofrendas*
– complex constructions that incorporate food, drink, photographs,
flowers, sweets and ceramic skulls – and decorations are usually
constructed. In the USA, where *Dia de los Muertos* is usually a single-
day celebration occurring on 2 November, large-scale celebrations
are popular in cities with significant Spanish-speaking populations,
and *ofrendas* may be presented in the context of an art competition.
Householders may also scatter the petals of a bright orange marigold
called *zempasuchitl* to mark a path for the spirits to follow, and they
might burn a fragrant resin known as *copal* to help the spirits return.

The writer and physician Frank Gonzalez-Crussi once inter-
viewed a woman who described her own mother walking into the
street outside her house on the afternoon of 2 November and greet-
ing the ghostly visitors:

Come in, blessed souls of my father, my mother, and my sisters. Please, come in. How did you do this year? Are you pleased with your living relatives? In the kitchen we have tamales, tostadas, pumpkin with honey, apples, oranges, sugarcane, chicken broth, a great deal of salt, and even a little tequila, so you may drink. Are you happy with what we have? My sons worked very hard this year so we could offer you this feast, as usual. Tell me, how is Saint Joseph? Did he receive the masses we ordered for him?[1]

In some areas, *Dias de los Muertos* includes a special night (usually 28 October) dedicated to those who died violently. On that particular evening, the food is placed outside the house to prevent any malignant spirits from entering.

Although much of the festival is devoted to the appreciation of family and food, it also playfully taunts Death by featuring bright, grinning skulls everywhere. These *calaveras* may be made from *alfeñique*, or sugar paste; they might be constructed from papier mâché or ceramic; or they might be paintings or drawings. The artist José Guadalupe Posada provided what has become the single most enduring image of *Dias de los Muertos*: 'La Catrina', a drawing of an elegant lady skeleton wearing a plumed hat, reminding us that Death reduces both rich and poor to bones.

*Dias de los Muertos* also has its own special ghost stories. The most popular focus on the young man who would rather spend his days drinking and carousing than honouring his dead parents; invariably, this thoughtless oaf is subjected to a terrifying visit from the enraged spirits and carried off to the land of the dead.

A more unusual story is that of Princess Mitzita and Prince Itzihuapa. This lovely tale comes from the village of Janitizio, on Lake Pátzcuaro, famed around the world for its elaborate and elegant Days of the Dead celebrations. This story dates back to the time when the Purepecha, the people who originally inhabited the area, were conquered by the Spanish. Princess Mitzita and her lover, Prince Itzihuapa, tried to obtain a legendary treasure buried at the bottom of the lake, hoping to use it to ransom Mitzita's captured father from the Spanish, but the youthful lovers were overcome by the ghostly warriors who guard the treasure. Now, on the Day of the Dead, Mitzita and Itzihuapa arise (along with the twenty spectral guards) to accept offerings.

A Mayan celebration known as *Hanal Pixan* probably also contributed heavily to *Dias de los Muertos*. Translating approximately as 'the soul's path through the essence of food', *Hanal Pixan* offers a number of unique traditional dishes and lasts for eight days. The first day is dedicated to the souls of children, who are offered sweets and a chicken stew. On 1 November the adult spirits arrive (a bowl of water and soap are set out so they can wash their hands first) and receive *mucbil* chicken, which requires days of preparation, including burying the meat in the earth. On the final day of *Hanal Pixan*, the visiting spirits are feted with a special tamale dish called *chachak-wa*.

Over the last few decades, the celebration of *Dias de los Muertos* has been the target of some controversy in Mexico, as Halloween has grown more popular there. Children (and their parents) enjoy the costumes and trick-or-treat ritual of Halloween, but conservative and religious commentators decry the loss of Mexico's own traditional celebration.

*Todos Santos* (All Saints' Day) and *Dia de Difuntos* (All Souls' Day) are celebrated through most of Central and South America, with some differences from the Mexican festival. In Ecuador and Peru, for example, the dead are honoured at the grave instead of in the home. Girls and unmarried women from Bolivia's Aymara people dance with dolls or other people's children in the hope of attracting the souls of dead children to ensure fertility. The Aymara also present the ghosts with ladders, to help them climb up out of Purgatory, and with boats, to aid them in travelling across nearby lakes.[2]

Contemporary Mexico is also home to some of the world's most tragic and frightening ghost legends, many of which have crossed the border into the United States with Mexican immigrants. These tales often paint a picture of the culture clash between Mesoamerican (Aztec) and European (Catholic) ways. In his book *Mexican Ghost Tales of the Southwest*, the writer and illustrator Alfred Avila includes such a story. 'The Bat' begins when the eponymous creature flies into a boy's bedroom one night, reveals itself to be the spirit of an Aztec warrior, and tells the boy:

> We the warriors who perished in battle are now forced to wander aimlessly in the darkness of the night. Our spirits can find no peace or rest, for there are neither temples to offer us sacrifices nor priests to ask our gods for favors.[3]

The bat/warrior tells the boy that it requires a slave guide of Spanish or mestizo blood, and has chosen the boy. The next day the boy is very ill; his mother tends him and prays, but he worsens. His mother seeks the help of a local *curandera*, or healer, who tells her that the boy has fallen under an ancient curse. The *curandera* is by the boy's side when the bat returns. Outraged by her presence, he tells her that he has the blessing of Mictlantecuhtli, the Aztec Lord of the Dead. The bat leaves before dawn since sunlight would destroy it, and the *curandera* prays to the Aztec gods for guidance in destroying the bat. The next night, when the bat returns, the *curandera* tricks it by gluing its feet down; then, just before sunrise, she demands to speak to Mictlantecuhtli, who appears and promises to take his bat and leave the boy alone. The story ends by suggesting that the boy grew up to become the famed revolutionary Pancho Villa.

A ghost known as La Japonesa ('the Japanese woman') is an example of one that travelled from rural Mexico to urban Los Angeles. The story tells of a Japanese urn that arrived in Mexico, full of cremated remains. When reports surfaced that the urn was haunted, a sailor deposited it in an isolated stand of desert cactus. Soon after, people in the vicinity started dying from vicious animal attacks; eventually it was discovered that the ghost of the Japanese woman whose ashes were in the urn was angry at being taken from her homeland and had taken the form of a gigantic, four-tailed cat-like creature. In the hills of El Monte, a suburb in the San Gabriel Valley not far to the east of Los Angeles, sightings of La Japonesa – complete with sketches – were reported on Internet chat boards in the early twentieth century.

*La Llorona* at the Plaza de Santa Catarina, Coyoacán.

However, no Mexican ghost legend is more famous than that of *La Llorona* (who could, in fact, be the single most famous ghost of the last few decades). This tale of filicide – a mother's deliberate murder of her own children – has been retold in dozens, possibly hundreds of variants. In perhaps the most classic version of the tale, *La Llorona* ('the wailing woman') is a widow with three small children; not content to play either grieving wife or mother (and more interested in drinking at the nearby tavern), one night she finally grows tired of her neglected, starving children's cries for food and drowns them in the river. After her own death, she is consigned to wander eternally near rivers, wailing over her fate and seeking more children to replace her own.

In other versions of the tale, *La Llorona* can appear as a ball of fire or a whirlwind; sometimes she can be seen only during the full moon, and cannot approach a church. Some claim she was a victim herself: that her husband came with the Spanish conquerors, fathered children with her and abandoned them all; and that she killed the children because they had Spanish blood. This variant of the story fuses *La Llorona* with La Malinche, the Aztec interpreter to and mistress of Hernán Cortés, who, legend has it, was abandoned by the conqueror after she bore him twin sons. When Cortés tried to return to Spain with his children, La Malinche stabbed them and threw them into a river, and soon thereafter became known as *La Llorona*.

The first reported sighting of *La Llorona* is often given as 1550 – about twenty years after La Malinche died. She was seen in Mexico City's Plaza Mayor, wearing the white dress and veil that would come to be associated with her, and more sightings soon appeared, usually at the full moon.

*La Llorona*'s tale has served for generations as both a warning to children against going out alone at night, and a caution to young women about choosing their men wisely, lest they find themselves abandoned with small mouths to feed. It has provided the basis for short stories, graphic novels, films and even amusement-park attractions – one of the most popular haunted mazes at Universal Studios' Halloween Horror Nights is the one known as *La Llorona*.

The Inca Empire, which once extended from Ecuador to Chile, practised human sacrifice that essentially created guardian ghosts. In 1621 a Spanish inquisitor, Hernández Príncipe, befriended the converted shaman in a Peruvian village where the inhabitants worshipped a goddess named Tanta Carhua. However, Príncipe soon learned the truth behind Tanta Carhua: in about 1430, an ambitious man named Caque Poma had offered his beautiful ten-year-old daughter, Tanta Carhua, for sacrifice to the sun. In return, the Inca emperor gave chieftainship of the village to Poma and deified Tanta. The villagers continued to consult Tanta for two centuries; they employed shamans, who went into a trance and allowed the spirit of Tanta to possess them, at which point they assumed a falsetto voice and answered questions about health or prosperity.[4]

The Tupari tribe in the Mato Grosso region of Brazil have a unique story to explain their dreams and why ghosts frequently appear in them: upon death, the spirit is blinded when its pupils vanish, and must fumble its way to the land of the dead. After travelling over the backs of giant crocodiles and serpents and encountering

frightening outsized jaguars, the *pabid*, as the blind spirit is called, arrives in the land of the dead, where its intestines are promptly eaten by fat worms. The *pabid* then meets Patobkia, the head magician of the village of the dead, who restores its sight, which allows the *pabid* to realize that it has died. The *pabid* live in round huts and eat food magically grown by Patobkia, and the Tupari magicians may visit the *pabid* village in their dreams. The Tupari also believe that each person possesses a second ghostly creature called a *ki-apoga-pod*, which bursts out of the heart a few days after burial. A magician feeds the creature, gives its unformed, clay-like face features and releases it into the air. If, however, the dead man was a magician, the *ki-apoga-pod* will stay in the village, eating and drinking, and providing the Tupari with dreams.[5]

Most of the ethnic groups and tribes of Africa practise some form of ancestor worship and believe that the deceased must receive proper burial or may return as angry ghosts. The Nyanga of Zaire (now the Democratic Republic of Congo) believe that those who die as a result of suicide or suspected sorcery return as restless spirits called *Binyanyasi*.[6]

Among the Yoruba, ghosts were thought to reside in a place called Deadland, and they had little knowledge of the affairs of humans. One Yoruba adage says: 'As grass cannot grow in the sky, so the dead cannot look out of the grave into the street.'[7] A Yoruba folk tale tells of a woman who gives a valuable necklace to a friend to hold for her; the second woman secretly places the necklace in a wall and covers the hole. Unfortunately she then dies, and when the owner of the necklace returns to ask for her property, she accuses the dead woman's two sons of stealing it. One of the boys is taken by the local chief and will be sold into slavery unless the necklace is returned, so the remaining son goes to the oracle and asks how he can find the necklace. The oracle tells him he must seek his mother in Deadland, which he can reach by doing the following:

> Let the child in search of his mother
> Offer an ebon sheep to the dead,
> When night falls in the grove of Ifa.

Let the child in search of his mother
Sprinkle his eyes with lustral water,
Then shall the dead be visible to him.

Let the child in search of his mother
Follow the shadows' noiseless footsteps,
So shall he reach the land of the dead.[8]

The boy is also instructed not to touch anybody he sees in Deadland. He follows the instructions, and finds his mother, and, when she reveals the hiding place of the necklace, is so overjoyed that he almost embraces her. His mother saves him by leaping back at the last instant, and the boy returns to the world of the living, retrieves the necklace and saves his brother.

The folklore of Africa's Yoruba people also formed the basis of the work of the internationally known writer Amos Tutuola. Tutuola's stories include goblins, witches, bizarre twists of fate, singing drums and ghosts. The title story in his collection *The Village Witch Doctor and Other Stories* adroitly plays on the way superstition can have disastrous consequences, and on the clash between traditional beliefs and contemporary scepticism. A witch doctor, Osanyin, has a friend named Aro, who inherits a great deal of money and tells Osanyin that he plans to bury it under a particular tree. Osanyin takes the money and blames Aro's dead father. Aro is forced into poverty, but marries and has a son, Ajaiyi, before he dies. Ajaiyi grows up poor, and, after accruing debts he can never repay, seeks Osanyin's help. Osanyin preys on Ajaiyi's credulity just as he did with his father, suggesting that if he places nine rams in sacks and leaves them on his father's grave, Aro's ghost will replace the rams with money. Ajaiyi can afford only six rams, which Osanyin takes, leaving the young man even poorer. Finally Osanyin tells Ajaiyi that he must provide the last three rams, but this time Ajaiyi hides in one of the sacks, planning to fight his father's ghost. When Osanyin steals the sacks, expecting them to hold rams, he is surprised to find Ajaiyi in one, holding a machete. Ajaiyi believes Osanyin to be the ghost of his father, and he nearly slays him, but at the last moment Osanyin returns the money to him.[9]

During the time when Europeans brought Africans as slaves to the New World, the beliefs of numerous ethnic groups – the Yoruba, Dahomeans, Congos, and so on – became melded with French Catholicism to form a new religion: Vodou. Vodou originated in Haiti, and incorporates ghosts into the pantheon of spirits (*loa* or *lwa*) that Vodouisants worship. Vodou is a three-tiered system, with a supreme god, *Bondye*, at the apex, dozens of demigods in the middle, and the spirits of deceased ancestors (*loa Ghede*) forming the base. Some of the demigods are believed to have a human origin: Papa Ghede, for example, is thought to be the first person who ever died. Now he is a powerful *loa* who oversees death and fertility, and also possesses an especially raucous sense of humour.

In the Jamaican religion of Kumina, each person is believed to possess a body, a soul-spirit and a *duppy*-ghost. Upon an individual's death, the soul-spirit ascends to Heaven, but separate rites must be performed for the *duppy*, or it may continue to haunt those nearby indefinitely. *Duppies* are dangerous and frightening entities:

> It sleeps during the day and roams the community at nights, lurking in dark alleys, abandoned buildings, and under trees, but must be back in its tomb before daybreak. Its feet never touch the ground (some are said to have feet with cow hooves); it talks with a clogged nasal accent, laughs in a shrill juvenile tone, and is able to count only to four.[10]

Protection from a *duppy* may be obtained by reciting the Lord's Prayer or counting past four.

Among the most interesting ghost traditions south of the equator are those of the Australian aborigines, who believe in the perpetual presence of ghosts in their lives. An early study of tribes in the western district of Victoria revealed the belief that each person possesses both a ghost and a wraith; the latter appears to them shortly before they die. At death, the ghost is believed to remain near the body for several days, but will vanish should anyone come close. It may approach friends of the dead person, and is occasionally glimpsed, although it disappears if its name is called. After three days, the ghost of a good person will ascend to a paradise above the clouds, where family waits and game is plentiful. The spirits of the evil, however, will wander the Earth for one year, causing fright and mischief, before descending to the hell of Ummekulleen, from which place they never return.[11]

In the mythology of most Australian aboriginal groups, the central concept is the 'Dreamtime' (sometimes also called the 'Dreaming'). Dreamtime involves the creation of the cosmos and, finally, of the world by the ancestors. Some groups believe that the Dreamtime was in the past, while others hold that it is simultaneously in the past and the present; in either case, it is possible to access the Dreamtime via dreams, with the help of ancestral spirits or dream spirits.[12]

It should come as no surprise that many of Australia's purportedly haunted spots nowadays are prisons (given Australia's history as a penal colony) or sites of aboriginal tragedies. Ned Kelly and more than 100 other convicts were hanged in Old Melbourne Gaol, and witnesses have reported disembodied voices and other paranormal activity there. More than 1,800 apparitions have been glimpsed at Port Arthur (once referred to as an 'inescapable prison'), and the Devil's Pool near Babinda, Queensland, is said to be home to the ghost of an aboriginal woman who drowned herself after being separated from her lover, and who now lures men to their death.[13]

# 6

# The Quest for Evidence: The Ghost and Science

In 1984 a fantasy-comedy called *Ghostbusters* struck box-office gold. The film starred Bill Murray, Dan Aykroyd and Harold Ramis as a trio of lovable nerds who applied their scientific acumen to the paranormal, using 'proton packs' and 'PKE meters' to track and capture pesky spirits.

Little did the makers of *Ghostbusters* know that their film would inspire real-life ghost-hunters, who stalk their elusive quarry with their own handheld measuring devices and high-tech equipment. As Amy Bruni of the television series *Ghost Hunters* said, 'I think Harold Ramis probably didn't realize the pedestal he and his *Ghostbusters* cast mates were put upon in the paranormal community. We worship that film.'[1]

Now, in the twenty-first century – with belief in supernatural happenings on the rise – anyone with a smartphone and a few pounds' worth of apps can call themselves a ghost-hunter. However, more serious paranormal investigators require more than this, and ghost-hunting is now big business, with companies all over the world providing increasingly complicated devices. Although the twenty-first-century ghost-hunter may still employ traditional techniques, including mediums (or 'sensitives'), dowsing rods (usually two narrow lengths of metal, which spirits are asked to cross to indicate 'no' and move apart for 'yes'), gathering eyewitness accounts and relying on 'bad feelings' or even physical effects like headaches, ghost-hunting now has a veneer of scientific plausibility. Many of the ghost-detection tools on the market operate on the popular notion

(Left to right) Bill Murray, Harold Ramis and Dan Aykroyd as the fully
equipped *Ghostbusters* (1984).

that ghosts are composed of a form of energy that falls within the
electromagnetic spectrum and can thus be read on measuring devices
that detect EMFs (electromagnetic frequencies). As one purveyor of
paranormal paraphernalia puts it, 'At a haunted location, strong,
erratic, fluctuating EMFs are commonly found. It seems these energy
fields have some definite connection to the presence of ghosts.'[2]
This belief that EMF correlates to spirit manifestations has its roots
in Spiritualism. 'I believe these singular manifestations are produced by the agency of spirits acting upon or using the magnetism
of the medium', said the Spiritualist supporter Newton Crosland
in 1873, in an attempt to explain séance phenomena like moving
tables or rapping sounds.[3] Even that greatest of inventors, Thomas
Edison, said in an interview in 1920,

> I have been at work for some time building an apparatus to
> see if it is possible for personalities which have left this earth
> to communicate with us ... If this is ever accomplished it will
> be accomplished, not by any occult, mystifying, mysterious,

or weird means, such as are employed by so-called 'mediums', but by scientific methods.[4]

A few minutes spent browsing Internet sites with names like 'ghoststop.com' will provide the newcomer with all the necessary tools. The ideal kit will include:

### K-II EMF meter (or safe range meter)

This small, plastic, handheld device operates from a single 9-volt battery and measures certain ranges of electromagnetic frequency. Although EMF meters were originally designed to assist electricians and others in locating power lines and other hidden electrical sources, paranormal investigators claim they can locate the low-frequency radiation emitted by spirits. The K-II has five LEDs that range from green (on the left side) to red, and 'spikes' are believed

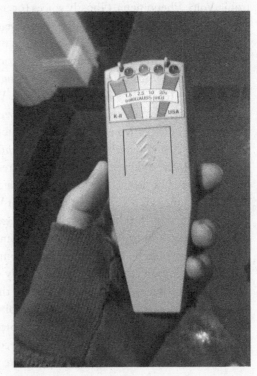

K-II EMF meter in use during a paranormal investigation.

to indicate the presence of ghosts. Ghost-hunters use the devices in two ways: 1) by looking for spikes in areas that are believed to be haunted; and 2) by asking ghosts to communicate via the meters, flashing the LEDs in response to questions. Kenny Biddle, a sceptic, tested a K-II under a variety of conditions and found that not only did the LEDs flash in response to mobile phones, cameras and his own body, but that the pressure switch – which must be continuously pressed down to keep the meter working – was easy to manipulate. Biddle concluded: 'There is no evidence to back up the claim that ghosts (however you may define them) have any effect on the electromagnetic field, or that any EMF meter has the ability to detect or be manipulated by a ghost.'[5]

## *Digital voice recorder*

These little handheld recorders are used to capture EVP, or Electronic Voice Phenomena. Ghostly voices (or mediums channelling spirits) have been caught in sound recordings for a century, and there are websites that host audio recordings of mediums in action and other paranormal phenomena dating back to the 1930s.[6] In the historical recordings, mediums, affecting various voices and accents, claim to speak as dead airmen, Oscar Wilde and Charlotte Brontë, among others. EVP was really popularized in 1968, when the Latvian psychologist Konstantin Raudive published *Breakthrough: An Amazing Experiment in Electronic Communication with the Dead*. Raudive claimed to hear the voices of dead relatives in recordings he had made of birdsong. In the 1970s the parapsychologist David Scott Rogo (and, a few years later, the novelist William Peter Blatty in *Legion*, the sequel to his best-seller *The Exorcist* of 1971) popularized the idea that the dead might try to communicate via phone and that they could be recorded in quiet rooms. Now, with digital audio technology, it has become increasingly easy to amplify and process recordings in a way that increases the gain (sensitivity) and sometimes reveals, among the white noise of a quiet recording, sounds that can resemble human voices speaking single words or short phrases. Parapsychologists recognize two forms of EVP: 1) Transform EVP, in which a discarnate entity is thought to use some of its energy to form words on an electronic medium; and 2) Opportunistic EVP, in which sounds are made available to the entities via a 'ghost box' (see below) or similar. Psychologists, however, are more likely to see EVP as a form of auditory pareidolia, a condition in which listeners interpret random sounds as voices speaking in the listener's language.

## Ovilus

This small electronic device (which, again, looks oddly like the Ghostbusters' PKE meter) reads environmental changes (mainly EMF) and converts the data into words, which are then both displayed as text on the device's screen and spoken via a small speaker (the Ovilus 4 even has several different voices available). Invented by the engineer Bill Chappell and offered through his website, the Ovilus (which he calls an ITC – Instrumental Trans Communication – device) operates under the theory that ghosts may be able to manipulate radiation to produce words, especially in answer to questions. The Ovilus includes a database of roughly 2,000 words and names, and is often likened to an electronic version of a Ouija board.

## Ghost (or spirit) box

Like the Ovilus, a ghost box is designed to facilitate spoken communication from discarnate entities. The ghost box may be a modified AM/FM radio, or it may be a device produced specifically for paranormal investigating; the basic principle is that it rapidly scans radio frequencies, producing a wave of white noise that is occasionally punctuated by a burst of sound. Some investigators believe that ghosts can transform the white noise into energy they can use to form words, which are spoken through the ghost box's speaker or headphones.

## Torches

Although the obvious use for a torch during a paranormal investigation would be to light the way through a dark, enclosed space, ghost-hunters use small torches as a means of communicating with ghosts. Such models measure about 2.5 x 15 cm (1 x 6 in.), and are easily turned on and off by twisting the lens at the front. Because this method of operation is simple and sensitive, investigators will often set several of these torches in place and ask any spirits who are present to turn one on and off; if two or more torches are used, the ghostly visitor may be asked specifically to manipulate only one of them, or to use different ones for different answers (for example, to use the blue torch to answer 'yes' and the red to answer 'no'). Because the torches are round and roll easily, spirits might also indicate their presence by physically moving them.

## Lasers

Like something straight out of a high-tech thriller, laser grids can now be set up anywhere to detect the presence of unearthly guests. For less than £70/$100, an investigator can purchase a laser-grid projector that claims to be able to measure 'speed [and] dimensions and even help us make a 3D model of the anomaly'.[7] Most investigators seem to prefer the green laser system, which projects hundreds of dots rather than lines. The laser is usually set up on a tripod with a video camera placed near by in order to capture any disturbance in the laser field.

## Thermometers

'Cold spots' have been recorded for centuries in haunted places, so ghost-hunters often employ digital thermometers to measure temperature fluctuations in a particular area. A sudden drop of several degrees is usually thought to indicate the approach or presence of a spirit.

## Thermal cameras

For the ghost-hunter with money to burn, a thermal camera might be the preferred equipment. As Steve Gonsalves of *Ghost Hunters* explains, a thermal camera 'allows you to see hot or cold spots in any location and track temperature fluctuations in real time. It is, without a doubt, one of the most valuable tools we use.'[8] A thermal camera tracks infrared radiation and translates it into a series of

THE QUEST FOR EVIDENCE: THE GHOST AND SCIENCE

predefined colours: hot objects show up as red, yellow or white, while cooler objects appear at the opposite end of the rainbow. Paranormal investigators believe that a thermal imaging camera may not only reveal 'temperature artefacts' created by a spirit's passage, but detect 'energy voids' (it is commonly accepted by ghost-hunters that discarnate entities suck energy from batteries and powered devices). As well as thermal imaging cameras, some investigators also use thermal sheets (sometimes marketed as 'ghost pads'), which react to changes in temperature by altering colour – preferably in the shape of a ghostly handprint.

### Apps

Apps are available that turn your phone into an EMF meter, an Ovilus device and even a thermal imaging accessory (the last was crowdfunded on Kickstarter as a practical tool to help resolve problems with home heating systems, but the fact that it went $175,000 past its goal of $20,000 may have had something to do with the popularity of thermal imaging in paranormal investigations). Certain ghost-hunting apps are less than practical, and in fact scientists and investigators both caution that many simply cannot do what a dedicated device can (an Ovilus phone app, for example, cannot collect EMF or temperature data, since a smartphone is not equipped with the appropriate detectors).

### Cameras

The amateur ghost-hunter can now use not just the still and video cameras on a smartphone, but also equipment capable of night vision and thermal imaging. Cameras may be used by human operators or set up to record in remote locations; they may be linked to motion detectors or simply left running. Images can later be enhanced using a computer.

Nearly 150 years before digital photography became ubiquitous, cameras were the first pieces of modern technology used to record ghosts. The first time a ghost was believed to have been captured on film occurred barely twenty years after the birth of practical photography, when in 1860 the New Jersey photographer W. Campbell took a photograph of an empty chair that, when developed, showed a small boy seated there. A year later the Boston engraver William Mumler took a self-portrait that also showed a ghostly figure whom Mumler identified as a long-dead cousin. Mumler was soon embraced by the Spiritualist movement, and by 1869 he had left his engraving job and moved to New York, where he charged high sums for his 'spirit photographs'. His most famous subject was a 'Mrs Lindall', who arrived at his studio one day and removed a heavy black veil to reveal that she was actually Mary Todd Lincoln, the widow of Abraham. Mumler's portrait of her did indeed show the figure of the late President bending down over her. After NYPD sent an undercover officer to sit for Mumler, he was arrested on charges of 'swindling credulous persons by what he called spirit photographs', and during the sensational trial testimony for the prosecution was given by the showman P. T. Barnum, who referred to the photos as 'humbug'.[9] However, the judge reluctantly found for the defence, citing a lack of evidence produced by the prosecution. In 1875 Mumler published a sort of autobiography, *The Personal Experiences of William H. Mumler in Spirit-photography*, in which he maintained his innocence yet failed to offer any explanation for why spirits should seek out his photographs to manifest themselves. Barnum, however, addressed spirit photographs in a chapter of his book *Humbugs of the World* in 1866:

> I need only explain the modus operandi of effecting this illusion, to make apparent to the most ignorant that no supernatural agency was required to produce photographs bearing a resemblance to the persons whose 'apparition' was desired. The photographer always took the precaution of inquiring about the deceased, his appearance and ordinary mode of wearing the hair. Then, selecting from the countless old 'negatives' the nearest resemblance, it was produced for the visitor in dim, ghostlike outline.[10]

While hoaxes were abundant during the height of the Spiritualism movement, a few amateur photographers caught images that

The Brown Lady of Raynham Hall, photographed by Indre Shira in 1936.

have defied explanation despite being studied for decades. In 1891 a woman named Sybell Corbet took a photo of the library at Combermere Abbey in Cheshire; the photograph required the shutter to be open for one hour, during which time no one entered the room. However, when the plate was developed, it showed what appeared to be a man seated in one of the library chairs – a man who was later identified as the late Lord Combermere. Perhaps even more convincing was the famed 'Brown Lady' photograph, taken on the staircase of Raynham Hall in Norfolk in 1936. The photographer, Indre Shira, turned his lens on the stairs when he spied the approaching apparition; even though his assistant saw nothing, the resulting image shows a transparent, shrouded figure descending, and remains perhaps the most mystifying ghost photograph of all time.

Famous ghost photographs have been captured in virtually every decade since the 1860s, and sometimes it has taken decades for the

Faked spirit photo showing famed conjurer J. N. Maskelyne as a ghost visiting the renowned sceptic Lionel Weatherly).

ghostly images to be debunked. Take, for example, a photograph depicting a figure known as the 'Wem Ghost'. In 1995 the amateur photographer Tony O'Rahilly shot the burning of the 90-year-old town hall in Wem, Shropshire; the photo later seemed to show an image of a little girl in period garb standing amid the flames. Locals suggested the ghost might belong to Jane Churm, a fourteen-year-old girl who died in a fire on the same spot in 1677. However, in 2010, when a local newspaper ran an article that reproduced a postcard of Wem from 1922, a local man named Brian Lear recognized a girl seen in the postcard as the 'Wem Ghost'. Residents who knew O'Rahilly, who had died in 2005, maintained his innocence even in the face of obvious proof of trickery. 'He always maintained that the picture was genuine and I believe him,' noted one local historian.[11]

The arrival of inexpensive and compact digital cameras in the late twentieth century created interest in a whole new type of photographed ghost, known as 'orbs'. A combination of factors inherent in digital cameras – including the short focal length of the lens and the close proximity of a built-in flash to the lens – can

Photograph taken in the service tunnel beneath the Stanley Hotel in Colorado showing orbs near the bottom.

highlight and magnify dust or water particles floating in the air just before the lens, producing transparent globes of light in photos. Because 'haunted' locations are likely to be dark enough to require the use of a flash, and also dusty or damp, they are likely to yield photos packed with orbs, which true believers may label 'spirit orbs' or even identify as 'a sign that angels are hovering nearby and the location is particularly blessed'.[12]

Recent technology has also provided easy access both to video cameras and to the mass sharing of videos through websites like YouTube. Occasionally videos that are purported to show ghosts are either convincing or entertaining enough to go 'viral', drawing hundreds of thousands of views in a short time. One posted in 2009 is still shared and discussed five years later, probably in part because of its (deliberately?) ironic setting. It claims to show a ghost walking away from Disneyland's Haunted Mansion, seen on four different security monitors as it leaves the queue area for the attraction, strolls through New Orleans Square and finally steps out on to the water (Rivers of America) bordering the area. The video, which is soundless, has generated over three million views and has been shared on dozens of paranormal blog and discussion sites. Speculation has ranged from a clever ad campaign on Disneyland's part to burn-in video anomalies, from old monitors to the ghost of Walt Disney himself patrolling his park.[13]

While most ghost-hunters are enthusiastic amateurs, there are nonetheless scientists in a variety of fields – medical doctors, physicists, engineers and even statisticians – who are conducting their own ghost hunts. These scientists are working in universities and laboratories in an attempt to explain one of mankind's oldest and most universal mysteries, with research methods that range from analysing historical data from the past to building new forms of testing equipment. Some of the leading theories include:

### *The power of suggestion*

In the television series *The X-Files*, FBI agent Fox Mulder had a poster behind his desk that featured the slogan 'I Want to Believe.'

Although Mulder's poster showed a flying saucer, it might just as easily have shown a ghost, as studies regarding the power of suggestion have demonstrated repeatedly that believers are likelier to experience paranormal activities than sceptics. The psychic researcher and psychoanalyst Nandor Fodor was among the first to investigate hauntings from the viewpoint of psychology, and in 1942 he suggested that 'the creepy atmosphere of an old house lends itself to an unconscious projection and dramatization of one's own conflicts into ghostly manifestations.'[14] In an experiment in 1997, James Houran and Rense Lange, researchers at the University of Illinois at Springfield, took 22 test subjects into an old theatre; half were told that the theatre was haunted, and the other half were told it was undergoing renovation. After analysing data collected from the participants, Lange and Houran concluded that 'the mere suggestion that a location is haunted [is] sufficient to produce poltergeist-like perceptions such as reports of a "sensed presence", apparitions, or other anomalous sensations.'[15] Similarly, when the psychologist Richard Wiseman conducted a study into alleged hauntings at Hampton Court Palace in London, he concluded not only that believers were likely to be more suggestible than sceptics, but that 'their sensations tended to focus on the type of scary-looking locations that are frequently featured in horror films.'[16] Other studies have suggested that our brains are constantly searching for meaning and explanation, and that this might explain our tendency to turn random sounds and small events into 'ghosts'. In 2009 the organizers of an attempt to create an artificially haunted room by using electromagnetic fields and infrasound concluded: 'The most parsimonious explanation for our findings is in terms of suggestibility.'[17]

*Stress*

Many psychological studies have shown that stressful situations amplify our detection of 'agents', or entities that cause things to happen. A person who is already alarmed will become more aware of stimuli; every creak or rattle creates fresh fear, leading to an ever-increasing state of anxiety. As Wiseman has noted, 'the process feeds on itself until the person starts to become highly agitated, anxious, and prone to more extreme sensations and hallucinations.'[18]

## Magnetic fields

At Laurentian University in Sudbury, Ontario, a specialist in 'neurotheology', Michael Persinger, has been conducting experiments in an attempt to demonstrate a link between magnetic fields and brain activity. Using a device that is sometimes referred to as the 'God helmet', Persinger fires weak magnetic fields into the brains of his subjects. He claims that 80 per cent of them experience some form of visual or auditory hallucination, or even have an encounter with God. Persinger says he has recorded high EMFs in houses where hauntings have been reported, and he believes his lab research has demonstrated a correlation between magnetic fields and paranormal phenomena; whether some people are more receptive to hallucinations caused by magnetic fields, or are more sensitive to the entities creating the fields, he isn't sure. Unfortunately, other scientists find more lacking in Persinger's research, claiming that they have been unable to replicate his results. A Swedish team, using double-blind scientific methods, found no difference between subjects who received the magnetic fields through the helmet and those who received nothing.

## Infrasound

Infrasound is low-frequency sound waves in the 0–20 Hz range; although sound in this range is inaudible to the human ear, it can affect other organs. For example, a NASA study listed the resonant frequency for the human eye at around 18 Hz, meaning that a sound at that frequency could cause visual hallucinations. Whole body vibration from infrasound may cause hyperventilation, and participants in experiments with infrasound have reported depression, dizziness and seeing objects move (from vibration). The researcher Vic Tandy first became aware of a correlation between infrasound and anomalous experiences when he was employed in a building where ghostly encounters seemed to be related to the installation of a new exhaust fan that produced infrasound waves. Tandy isolated a standing wave of 19 Hz that corresponded to the exact location where most of the phenomena had been reported, and when the mount of the fan was modified, the 'ghost' was exorcized.[19] The ghosts-as-sound-waves theory also works well in old buildings, where thicker walls resonate better, and where there may be little furniture present to absorb sound waves. However, further experiments subjecting people to standing waves of 19 Hz have failed to produce the desired results.

### Temporal lobe epilepsy

This form of epilepsy can cause seizures, hallucinations and intense feelings. Michael Persinger and Sandra Tiller were once running a routine EEG scan on a female patient when the subject reported a presence in the room; when the doctors examined the scan results, they noticed a significant spike in activity in her left temporal lobe at the time when she reported the presence. Dr Manuel Varquez Caruncho has suggested that the nineteenth-century composer Chopin – who reported ghostly sightings and even once saw a variety of entities crawling from his piano – may have suffered from temporal lobe epilepsy.[20]

Chopin and his 'ghosts', postcard, 19th century.

## Other physical ailments

Sleep deprivation, hypnagogic states, drugs and even carbon monoxide poisoning have all been linked to ghost sightings. During hypnagogic states – the time between wakefulness and sleep (or, when going from sleep to wakefulness, hypnopompic) – the brain can become confused as it moves into or out of the dream world, and this might explain why ghosts are so often reported at bedsides. Similarly, sleep paralysis explains many bedroom ghost visitations, and the commonly heard accompaniment of being unable to move. Because our muscles are paralysed during dream states (to prevent us from injuring ourselves by acting out the movements of our dreams), awakening suddenly from an REM state can lead to the sensation of being paralysed, while moving abruptly from a dream into wakefulness may result in hallucinations. This condition is sometimes called 'Old Hag Syndrome', since many sufferers describe finding a horrible old crone perched on their bed or even on their

Sleep paralysis in action: Henry Fuseli's *The Nightmare*,
first exhibited in 1782.

chest (and since it was once believed that witches 'rode the backs' of their victims).

As a final word on scientific investigation into the age-old mystery of ghosts, then, it seems that while science has been unable to prove the existence of ghosts, it has also been unable to provide a satisfactory alternative explanation for such phenomena. The hunt continues.

# 7

# From King Richard to
# *Paranormal Activity*: The Ghost
# in Literature, Film and
# Popular Culture

If we can concede that the modern fictive ghost story started when Hamlet was visited by his late father and nearly a dozen spectres urged Richard III to 'despair and die', there remains one more question, similar to that which surrounds the word 'ghost' itself: how do we define the ghost story? It is not as easy as it might at first seem. For example, Fitz-James O'Brien's short story 'What Was It?' of 1859 is often classified as an early example of the ghost tale, but there's not a ruined abbey nor a shimmering, translucent figure bent on revenge to be (un)seen. The story centres on a man who is attacked one night by an invisible creature of some sort, which he manages to capture and hold prisoner until it weakens and dies. At the end of the story, he buries it in the garden of his boarding house, knowing that he will never resolve the mystery of what it was.

Even F. Marion Crawford's 'The Upper Berth' (1886), which is almost invariably included in anthologies of classic ghost stories, seems to defy categorization as such, focusing not on an undead spectre, but on a mysterious marine entity that haunts one cabin of a ship. S. T. Joshi, a horror genre scholar and expert in the weird tale, has noted that 'the ghost story as such does not allow very much room for expansion or originality.'[1] M. R. James, whose collection *Ghost Stories of an Antiquary* (1904) places him in the very top rank of ghost-tale writers, had some concrete thoughts on what made a good work of ghost fiction:

Slimer from *Ghostbusters* (1984) – surely the star of the show.

as a rule, the setting should be fairly familiar and the majority of the characters and their talk such as you may meet or hear any day. A ghost story of which the scene is laid in the twelfth or thirteenth century may succeed in being romantic or poetical: it will never put the reader into the position of saying to himself, 'If I am not very careful, something of this kind may happen to me!' Another requisite, in my opinion, is that the ghost should be malevolent or odious: amiable and helpful apparitions are all very well in fairy tales or in local legends, but I have no use for them in a fictitious ghost story. Again, I feel that the technical terms of 'occultism,' if they are not very carefully handled, tend to put the mere ghost story (which is all that I am attempting) upon a quasi-scientific plane, and to call into play faculties quite other than the imaginative.[2]

Oddly, James does not state the obvious: that the tale should include a ghost (although he does mention 'The Upper Berth' as a ghost story). Perhaps the definition of 'ghost' was flexible enough for James to extend it to any supernormal creature that could not be easily explained. Similarly, in her often-quoted study *Night Visitors: The Rise and Fall of the English Ghost Story*, Julia Briggs notes:

'ghost story' . . . can denote not only stories about ghosts, but about possession and demonic bargains, spirits other than those of the dead, including ghouls, vampires, werewolves, the 'swarths' of living men and the 'ghost-soul' or *Doppelgänger*.[3]

For the purposes of a book that is a history of ghosts, discussion here will be limited to those stories that centre on ghosts, and not on other creatures of the night. Given that classical works and folklore have already been discussed in earlier passages, this section will delineate the ghost in literature (and, later, cinema and other art forms) from 1764 onwards.

Fortunately, all historians and critics of the ghost story agree in choosing that date, since it was the year of release of Horace Walpole's novel *The Castle of Otranto*, which not only inaugurated the ghost novel, but also began the cycle of Gothic literature in which ghosts often figured so prominently.

After a stunningly surreal opening in which a sickly young bridegroom is crushed by a giant helmet that seemingly falls from nowhere, much of *Otranto* is given over to melodramatic scheming as Manfred, the lord of the castle, plots to marry the young princess Isabella himself after his son Conrad is killed by the mysterious helmet. When Isabella's father, Frederic, arrives at the castle, he falls in love with Manfred's daughter Mathilda, but is warned away from marrying her by a fearsome ghost. The encounter with the ghost, who first seems to be a monk kneeling in prayer, is possibly the book's most overtly horrific scene: 'the figure, turning slowly round, discovered to Frederic the fleshless jaws and empty sockets of a skeleton, wrapt in a hermit's cowl.'[4] That image comes fairly late in the story, but it would influence the horror and Gothic genres for centuries.

The greatest practitioner of the Gothic story is generally reckoned to have been Ann Radcliffe, whose work was held in such esteem that creators like the poet Keats referred to her as 'Mother Radcliffe'. Her works have been continuously in print for more than 200 years. Her finest work is probably *The Mysteries of Udolpho* (1794), which firmly established most of the tropes of the Gothic novel: the beleaguered heroine, the wicked aristocrat, the virtuous hero, the travelogue and, of course, the ghosts. Radcliffe's skill is obvious in this passage, when the heroine's servant, Annette, describes an eerie encounter:

> 'I had heard strange stories of that chamber before,' said Annette: 'but as it was so near yours, ma'amselle, I would not tell them to you, because they would frighten you. The servants had told me, often and often, that it was haunted, and that was the reason why it was shut up: nay, for that matter, why the whole string of these rooms, here, are shut up. I quaked whenever I went by, and I must say, I did sometimes think I heard odd noises within it. But, as I said, as I was passing along the corridor, and not thinking a word about the matter, or even of the strange voice that the Signors heard the other night, all of a sudden comes a great light, and, looking behind me, there was a tall figure, (I saw it as plainly, ma'amselle, as I see you at this moment), a tall figure gliding along (Oh! I cannot describe how!) into the room, that is always shut up, and nobody has the key of it but the Signor, and the door shut directly.'[5]

Oddly, throughout Radcliffe's body of work, which includes such other Gothic gems as *The Italian* and *The Romance of the Forest*, there are no real ghosts – instead, every ghostly occurrence is explained away rationally by the novel's ending. Perhaps Radcliffe was merely expressing the 'contemptuous skepticism of the last age' that Catherine Crow would decry 50 years later in *The Night-side of Nature*.

Matthew 'Monk' Lewis may be best known as the author of the Gothic classic *The Monk* (1796), which features a ghostly nun (among other supernatural goings-on), but for many critics his real contribution to the ghost story and to Gothic literature was as editor of the anthology *Tales of Wonder* (1801). This two-volume survey is notable for, among other achievements, presenting early work by Walter Scott, who may be the real inventor of the short ghost story. Scott's work in *Tales* includes the ballad 'The Eve of Saint John', about a spectral knight who continues to visit his lady love after his death, but it is Scott's story 'The Tapestried Chamber' of 1831 that stands as one of the first important ghost stories, if not *the* first. In the second paragraph of the story, Scott seems almost dismissive of his work when he states that 'it must be admitted that the particular class of stories which turns on the marvellous possesses a stronger influence when told than when committed to print.'[6] Scott proceeds to offer a tale that combines many of the stories called 'true accounts' that proliferated about this time, and in the process establishes most of the tropes of the ghost-story form. 'The Tapestried Chamber' is about a general returning home from a war who stops for a rest at old Woodville Castle. During the night, he has a startling encounter:

> I was suddenly aroused by a sound like that of the rustling of
> a silken gown, and the tapping of a pair of high-heeled shoes,
> as if a woman were walking in the apartment. Ere I could
> draw the curtain to see what the matter was, the figure of a
> little woman passed between the bed and the fire. The back of
> this form was turned to me, and I could observe, from the
> shoulders and neck, it was that of an old woman, whose dress
> was an old-fashioned gown.[7]

When the woman turns, her face is terrifying – corpse-like and evil – and even the courageous military man is shaken. Later that day the general spots a portrait of the woman he saw, and his host confesses that the woman is a 'wretched ancestress' who was guilty of many vile crimes.

Scholars label the period between 1840 and 1920 as a golden age for the ghost story, and it is probably no coincidence that this time frame roughly parallels the rise and fall of Spiritualism. If we discount Edgar Allan Poe, who wrote no ghost stories (although some critics debate whether his piece 'Ligeia' can be called a ghost story or not), then the first great author of this new golden age must surely have been J. Sheridan Le Fanu. Le Fanu is often credited with being one of the originators of the vampire story (thanks to his novella *Carmilla* of 1871), but he was also a skilled purveyor of

Hand-coloured etching depicting the appearance of Marley's Ghost, from Charles Dickens's *A Christmas Carol*, illustrated by John Leech in 1843.

ghost stories who undoubtedly advanced the sub-genre, thanks to such works as 'Aungier Street' (1853). The opening line of that story echoes Scott's earlier suggestion that ghost tales are better when conveyed orally: 'It is not worth telling, this story of mine – at least, not worth writing.'[8] The story follows two young men who take up residence in an abandoned house (rent-free), and Le Fanu ably shows the way in which ghostly fascination often attaches itself to antiquated structures:

There had been very little done in the way of modernising details; and, perhaps, it was better so; for there was something queer and by-gone in the very walls and ceilings – in the shape of doors and windows – in the odd diagonal site of the chimney-pieces – in the beams and ponderous cornices – not to mention the singular solidity of all the woodwork, from the banisters to the window-frames, which hopelessly defied disguise, and would have emphatically proclaimed their antiquity through any conceivable amount of modern finery and varnish.[9]

The story echoes Scott's 'Tapestried Chamber' in presenting, in a haunted room, an encounter that is resolved by the protagonist's glimpse of a portrait. Unlike the earlier tale, however, it is lengthy, with a carefully executed build-up of suspense and mood.

In 1843 a novelist best known for his episodic dramas produced what is not only the most famous ghost story of the nineteenth century, but also possibly the most famous ghost story of *any* century: *A Christmas Carol* by Charles Dickens is also, of course, the best-loved Christmas story ever written, and offers a pointed look at economic disparity and greed. The plot – in which the miserly Ebenezer Scrooge is visited by a variety of phantoms one Christmas night – hardly needs recounting, but it is worth revisiting the initial appearance of the ghost of Scrooge's former partner, Marley:

At this the spirit raised a frightful cry, and shook its chain with such a dismal and appalling noise, that Scrooge held on tight to his chair, to save himself from falling in a swoon. But how much greater was his horror, when the phantom taking off the bandage round its head, as if it were too warm to wear indoors, its lower jaw dropped down upon its breast![10]

Compare this to classical descriptions 2,000 years earlier of chain-rattling ghosts.

Over the remainder of the nineteenth century, ghost stories filled the pages of popular magazines and cheap books; standouts were provided by Wilkie Collins, Charlotte Riddell and Vernon Lee (Violet Paget). One of the finest works produced that century was also one of the last: Henry James's novella *The Turn of the Screw* (1898), which twisted the ghost story with psychological insights and ambiguous events. The story of an unnamed governess to two small children, Miles and Flora – who may be haunted by the ghosts of the last governess, Miss Jessel, and her lover, Peter Quint – is rife with suggestions of child molestation and sexual tension. The novella is also notable for being one of the first to refer directly to earlier works: 'Was there a "secret" at Bly – a mystery of Udolpho or an insane, an unmentionable relative kept in unsuspected confinement?'[11]

The arrival of the new century saw a fresh crop of master fantasists spinning ghost stories. Arthur Machen, Edith Wharton, Walter de la Mare, Mary Wilkins Freeman, Oliver Onions, Lord Dunsany, Ambrose Bierce, Algernon Blackwood and, of course, M. R. James all contributed works that are still read and enjoyed to this day. By 1920, however, the ghost-story cycle had run its course. Spiritualism was dying out, and cinema seemed to be the preferred way to experience flickering shadows. The pulp writers of the 1930s, '40s and '50s certainly wrote of ghosts on occasion, although such writers as H. P. Lovecraft and Robert E. Howard were more interested in exploring the cosmic horror of elder gods and heroic fantasy. In 1941 Theodore Sturgeon, who is probably known mostly as the author of such science-fiction classics as *More Than Human* (1953), wrote a short story called 'Shottle Bop' that not only started the 'odde shoppe' sub-genre of fantasy stories, but also suggested that a man who could see ghosts might also see the parts of ghosts severed in accidents.

It was in 1959, however, that a novel considered by many to be one of the greatest ghost stories ever written appeared. In the opening of Shirley Jackson's *The Haunting of Hill House*, she captures the disturbing loneliness of the haunted house in a way that no other writer had done before:

> No live organism can continue for long to exist sanely under conditions of absolute reality; even larks and katydids are

Ghosts in pulp fiction: cover of *Avon Ghost Reader* (1946).

supposed, by some, to dream. Hill House, not sane, stood by itself against its hills, holding darkness within; it had stood so for eighty years and might stand for eighty more. Within, walls continued upright, bricks met neatly, floors were firm, and doors were sensibly shut; silence lay steadily against the wood and stone of Hill House, and whatever walked there, walked alone.[12]

Just as Henry James had done in *The Turn of the Screw* some 60 years earlier, Jackson invested the ghost story with a superbly realized psychological portrait of a troubled woman whose tenuous hold on reality crumbles in the face of paranormal happenings. *The Haunting of Hill House* was also one of the first books to make extensive use of a scientific investigation of the paranormal, in its story of a scientist who, accompanied by two 'sensitives' and the house's young male owner, takes up residence in search of evidence of the paranormal. Jackson wrote the book after awakening one morning to find a cryptic note on her desk. It read simply 'DEAD DEAD', and after seeing the note – which she had no memory of having written – Jackson said: 'I had no choice. The ghosts were after me.'[13] The book was nominated for the National Book Award, and has been called 'the greatest haunted house story ever written'.[14]

The writer Richard Matheson was already an established novelist (having written the grandfather of all zombie books, *I Am Legend*, in 1954) when he decided to write a haunted-house book. He was greatly inspired by what Jackson had achieved in *The Haunting of Hill House*, and was also a fan of real hauntings, having amassed a large personal library of non-fiction accounts. In 1971 he combined these interests to produce *Hell House*, the story of a team of scientific investigators and mediums investigating the chilling Belasco mansion. Matheson's novel added a considerable portion of sex and gore to the ghost-story formula, although Matheson claimed in interviews: 'None of the incidents in the book were made up by me. They had all happened in various haunted houses around the world.' He also mentioned that he had taken events from the Borley Rectory haunting (see chapter Three), and that the house's physical layout was inspired by Hearst Castle.[15]

In the 1970s the popularity of the horror genre exploded, owing to the success of the books and films of *The Exorcist* and *Jaws*, and also thanks to a novelist who had his first success in 1974 with a novel about a telekinetic teenager named Carrie. If *The Haunting of Hill House* is the critical favourite for the greatest ghost story ever written, then Stephen King's third novel, *The Shining* (1977), just might be the most popular. As we saw in chapter Three, the novel's gestation began on the night that King and his wife, Tabitha, decided to stay at a massive old resort hotel high in the Colorado Rockies, the Stanley Hotel. It was towards the end of the main season for the hotel, which shut down during the cold, snowy winters, and the couple were almost the only guests. King experienced a number of strange things in the hotel, especially in Room 217, where he and Tabitha were staying. The next morning he had the basic outline for the story of a recovering alcoholic named Jack Torrance who agrees to act as caretaker of a seasonal resort hotel. Jack brings his wife, Wendy, and young son Danny to the hotel, where they will have almost no contact with the outside world until the arrival of spring. Danny possesses 'the shining' – psychic abilities that allow him to see all the Overlook Hotel's ghostly residents – and the winter turns progressively worse as the ghosts shake Jack's sobriety and sanity. King's description of a dead woman whom Danny sees rising from a bath remains one of the most visceral and frequently imitated depictions of a ghost in literature:

The woman in the tub had been dead for a long time. She was bloated and purple, her gas-filled belly rising out of the cold, ice-rimmed water like some fleshy island. Her eyes were fixed on Danny's, glassy and huge, like marbles. She was grinning, her purple lips pulled back in a grimace. Her breasts lolled. Her pubic hair floated. Her hands were frozen on the knurled porcelain sides of the tub like crab claws.[16]

Two years after *The Shining* Peter Straub returned the ghost story to the realm of the vengeance-seeking spectre with his critically praised novel *Ghost Story*, in which characters ask one another:

'What's the worst thing you've ever done?' In contrast to King's description of a ghost, which emphasizes its appearance and physicality, Straub's spectres are sometimes furious, but often pathetic:

> his mother was washed of life, too empty even for despair. She seemed animated only by need – need at a level beneath all feeling ... Peter began to cry. They were eerie, not frightening. Standing out there below his window, so pitiably drained, they were as if merely dreamed.[17]

Although serial killers and zombies seem to have dominated the horror-novel market over the years since Straub's and King's books, there are still writers who have been exploring and expanding the ghost story. Mark Z. Danielewski's *House of Leaves* (2000) experimented with a format that included footnotes and unusual page layouts, and the book almost immediately garnered a cult following; Alice Sebold's surprise bestseller *The Lovely Bones* (2002) was embraced by Spiritualists for its depiction of a non-religious afterlife, from which a murdered teenage girl comments on her former life and family; and Sarah Langan's award-winning *Audrey's Door* (2009) brought both a feminist and an urban sensibility to the tried-and-true genre.

Ghosts have also figured prominently in several popular new genres and sub-genres: paranormal romance has added more eroticism (and creatures) to the Gothic romance formula; urban fantasy features tough female protagonists who may be in conflict with, assisted by or romantically involved with a ghost; the young adult fantasies of such authors as J. K. Rowling (*Harry Potter*) and Joseph Delaney (*The Spook's Apprentice*) make liberal use of spectres; the weird western mixes ghosts, magic and other paranormal oddities with Old West gunslingers; graphic novels have revitalized ghostly superheroes like The Spectre and Ghost Rider; and, as more Japanese *manga* are translated into English, American audiences have discovered series like *Ghost Talker's Daydream* and the gruesome, socially conscious works of the writer and artist Hideshi Hino (*Panorama of Hell*).

Ghosts from Méliès' *Le Manoir du Diable* (1896).

If the evolution of the literary ghost can be seen as moving largely from shadowy, incommunicative spectre to psychologically observed and deeply explored character, almost the reverse seems true in cinema, where the undead spirit has moved from the chatty and urbane to increasingly violent, speechless force of nature.

It is perhaps telling of the ghost's cinematic future that the first ghost film was made by the man who is often thought of as the father of special effects, the French director and magician Georges Méliès. His short film *Le Manoir du Diable* (*The Devil's Castle*, 1896) was made just two years after the first motion picture, *Sortie de l'usine Lumière de Lyon* (*Workers Leaving the Lumière Factory in Lyon*), and – as with most early Méliès films – is mainly a whimsical, light-hearted way for a magician in a new medium to present his tricks (which mainly consist of actors suddenly appearing or disappearing). The plot is simple: two wayfarers accidentally stumble into the Devil's own castle, and the Devil calls forth bats, imps, witches and ghosts to confuse and attack them. The film – one of hundreds made by Méliès – was thought to be lost until 1988, when a copy was found in the New Zealand Film Archives. Now film historians consider it both the first ghost film and the first horror film.

Original poster from *The Uninvited* (1944).

Oddly enough, the cycle of Universal horror films, which began in 1923 with the studio's *Hunchback of Notre Dame* and reached its apex in the 1930s with such classics as *Frankenstein, Dracula* and *The Mummy*, never produced a ghost film. The closest it came was with the black-humoured *The Old Dark House* (1932), which explored the notion of the isolated, gloomy mansion where young travellers are forced to seek shelter, but filled the house with human antagonists.

It wasn't until the late 1930s and '40s that ghosts became popular on the silver screen, and at that point they were mostly comic or romantic leads; in fact, films like *Here Comes Mr Jordan* (1941) and *Between Two Worlds* (1944) were so light that the film scholar Peter Valenti characterized them as 'film blanc', in contrast to 'film noir': 'The film *blanc* shows contemporary Americans successfully negotiating a return to the real mortal world after a trip to the twilight region between life in the physical world and either death or an altered state of existence in another spiritual world.'[18] Other ghost films from this era – specifically the Topper series (which began with *Topper* in 1937) and *The Ghost and Mrs Muir* (1947) – leaned towards the comedic and romantic.

In many respects, *The Uninvited* (1944) was the first real ghost film. It featured a story that readers of ghost literature will recognize: two siblings, Rick (Ray Milland) and Pamela (Ruth Hussey), purchase Windsor House, an old mansion situated on a rocky bluff along the coast of Cornwall. After encountering cold spots, mysterious draughts and disembodied sobbing voices, Rick and Pamela realize their new house is haunted. The haunting somehow centres on the young Stella (Gail Russell) and her relationship with her late mother, who is revealed as the spirit haunting Windsor House. A mystery regarding Stella's past is resolved, and at the end Rick confronts the apparition of Stella's mother, thus ending the haunting. Although the film's frights pale by comparison to later movies, it has influenced such directors as Martin Scorsese, who called it one of the eleven scariest movies ever made and praised it because 'the tone is very delicate, and the sense of fear is woven into the setting, the gentility of the characters.'[19]

Although horror films of the 1950s tended more towards giant monsters and menacing extraterrestrials, the decade did produce one ghost film that remains a terrifying youthful memory for many modern film lovers: William Castle's *House on Haunted Hill* of 1959. Featuring a delightfully camp performance from Vincent Price as a millionaire who has challenged five guests to spend the night in a rented haunted house, the film is perhaps the classic example of the ghost-hoax sub-genre, in which the various manifestations and occurrences are revealed at the end to be an elaborately staged hoax. Castle, an acknowledged master at film promotion, released *House on Haunted Hill* with 'Emergo', a plastic skeleton flown on a wire over the heads of the viewers. The film is also notable for using one of the most unusual locations ever for its haunted house: Frank Lloyd Wright's famed Ennis House was shot for the exteriors.

In the early 1960s were released two of the finest examples of the ghost film ever produced (and it is no coincidence that both were based on literary classics): Jack Clayton's *The Innocents* (1961, based on *The Turn of the Screw*) and Robert Wise's *The Haunting* (1963, based on *The Haunting of Hill House*). Both films explored the sexuality of the female protagonists and relied on simple effects and sinister atmosphere, and although both were only moderately successful upon initial release, both are now considered among the most frightening ghost films of all time. *The Haunting* in particular has achieved the status of a major influence on the genre.

In the 1970s, as the popularity of horror exploded in book-shops, only one ghost film was a significant success: *The Amityville Horror* (1979), based on Jay Anson's book. Starring James Brolin and Margot Kidder as the beleaguered Lutzes, the film was poorly received by critics, but a box-office success. A whopping fifteen films related to *The Amityville Horror* have been released, making it the most filmed ghost franchise in film history.

One other film from the 1970s is worth mentioning, despite its lack of popular or critical success: *The Legend of Hell House* (1973), an adaptation of Richard Matheson's novel *Hell House*. Matheson wrote the screenplay himself, and unfortunately reduced the book's sex and violence by such a significant amount that little but the

French/German poster for *The Innocents* (1961).

(slightly threadbare) basic plot was left. The film is interesting, however, for being possibly the first to feature a scene of a medium (played by Pamela Franklin) producing ectoplasm during a trance.

During the 1980s cinemas were filled with a new sub-genre: the slasher film, which typically consisted of an implacable antagonist pursuing shrieking, oversexed teenagers (and a 'final girl' who survived thanks to a combination of determination, intelligence and her refusal to engage in casual sex). It is not completely implausible to suggest that slashers functioned in much the way ghost stories had in the past: they presented an anti-hero who acted on pure rage, was often acting out vengeance against perceived wrongs, and was nearly impossible to thwart. In the case of one highly successful slasher series – *A Nightmare on Elm Street* – the killer was a ghost returned from the grave to haunt the dreams (another classic ghost trope) of the children whose parents (note the ancestral link) had murdered him.

However, more traditional ghost films were still being made. In 1980 and 1981 three were produced that were based on recent novels: *The Shining*, *Ghost Story* and *The Entity*. Arguably the least successful of these is the second, adapted by the director John Irvin from Peter Straub's novel of the same name, and derided by the critic Vincent Canby as 'a very dim pleasure'.[20] *The Entity*, which was delayed from release until 1982, offered a solid adaptation (anchored by a superb lead performance by Barbara Hershey) of Frank De Felitta's novel, which was based on the Doris Bither case investigated by UCLA's Parapsychology Laboratory (see chapter Three). Scorsese has labelled this another of his 'scariest movies of all time', and praised the film, noting: 'The banal settings, the California-modern house, accentuate the unnerving quality.'[21]

Stanley Kubrick's adaptation of Stephen King's *The Shining* generated one of the more controversial adaptations, dividing fans and critics alike along love it-or-hate it lines. Roger Ebert gave the film his highest rating, but said: 'The movie is not about ghosts but about madness.'[22] *Variety* excoriated the film: 'The crazier Nicholson gets, the more idiotic he looks. Shelley Duvall transforms the warm sympathetic wife of the book into a simpering, semi-retarded hysteric.'[23] King himself famously hates the film, and says that he had a phone conversation in which Kubrick explained why he wasn't frightened by ghost stories: 'I think stories of the supernatural are fundamentally optimistic, don't you? If there are ghosts

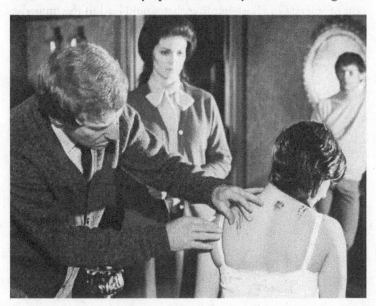

Barrett (Clive Revill) checks wounds in *The Legend of Hell House* (1973).

then that means we survive death.'[24] However, a study in 2013, which combined a poll with actual heart-rate monitoring of viewers watching horror films, measured *The Shining*'s 'Here's Johnny!' shock as the most frightening scene ever (with a 28.2 per cent jump in pulse speed).[25]

A film released in 1982, however, became one of the most influential in history by applying new special-effects technology to the ghost film: *Poltergeist*. The story of a suburban family beset by an especially kinetic haunting was praised by critics for its energy and build-up of tension, but audiences found the dynamic, showy special effects equally (or even more) enthralling. Five years after *Star Wars* redefined film effects, applying those filmic tricks to a ghost story was a sure-fire formula for success, and *Poltergeist* was the top-grossing horror film of 1982.

Two years later, as we saw in chapter Six, a different kind of ghost film would have an impact that was felt beyond cinemas: *Ghostbusters* not only paved the way for later ghost comedies such as *Beetlejuice* (1988), but also planted the seeds for the real-life explosion of interest in ghost-hunting that would lead to the immense success of reality television shows and ghost tourism. *Ghostbusters*

Extreme paranormal activity in *Poltergeist* (1982).

Dana (Sigourney Weaver) and Louis (Rick Moranis)
possessed in *Ghostbusters* (1984).

also spawned sequels, a cartoon series and a merchandising bonanza of toys and collectibles. A reboot starring an all-female team is scheduled for release in 2016.

In 1990 a ghost film was not only the year's top-grosser, but also earned an Academy Award nomination for Best Film: *Ghost*, starring Patrick Swayze as the eponymous lead, Demi Moore as the endangered girlfriend whom he tries to help, and Whoopi Goldberg as the reluctant medium who is shocked to find that her skills are real. The film combined New Age metaphysics (or old-style Spiritualism) with romance and suspense, and quotes such as 'The love inside, you take it with you', endeared it to audiences worldwide. *Ghost* was also adapted for the London and Broadway stages in 2011 and 2012.

By the end of the 1990s, however, the ghosts were back to scare with two very different films, both of 1999: *The Sixth Sense* brought a feeling of serious drama to an unnerving tale of a boy (Haley Joel Osment) with psychic abilities, who is aided by a sympathetic counsellor (Bruce Willis) with a (not so) secret. The big surprise,

The ghostly Sam (Patrick Swayze, centre) watches medium Oda Mae (Whoopi Goldberg) at work in *Ghost* (1990).

though, was a film with a budget of less than $25,000 that earned $250 million worldwide, and launched the craze for 'found footage' films: *The Blair Witch Project*. The film claims to be the recovered videotape of three student filmmakers who have disappeared, and shows the teens venturing into a supposedly haunted forest to make a documentary. The filmmakers, Daniel Myrick and Eduardo Sanchez, employed three unknown actors, gave them video cameras and spent eight days with them in Seneca Creek State Park in Maryland; the actors not only shot the film, but improvised their lines. Although it was well received by critics, the picture owed much of its astonishing success to the first Internet marketing campaign, which treated the subject-matter as completely real and created a buzz well in advance of the film's actual release.

During the first decade of the new millennium, cinematic horror was dominated by 'torture porn' – quickly made, excessively bloody films that emphasized torture and sadism. For a while, American ghost films seemed to be confined to remakes of Japanese successes – *The Ring, The Grudge, Dark Water*. Even *The Others* of 2001 – an elegant, spooky ghost film starring Nicole Kidman, and with a considerable debt to *The Turn of the Screw* – was essentially a Spanish film with an English-speaking cast.

In the second half of the 2000s, as box-office receipts on 'torture porn' films began to ebb, ghost films made a strong return, with a slew of releases that included *The Messengers, Paranormal Activity, The Haunting in Connecticut, Insidious, The Conjuring* and a slew of sequels. One film stood apart from the others, mainly because of provenance: *The Woman in Black* (2012) was not only based on Susan Hill's acclaimed novella of 1983 (which had spawned both an earlier television adaptation, by Nigel Kneale, and a long-running stage play), but produced by the venerable Hammer Films, which had its biggest U.S. opening ever with the film.

Ghost films are enjoyed and produced around the world, and subtitled films are often easier to find than translated books. Japan in particular has a fine history of cinematic apparitions, beginning in 1953 with Kenji Mizoguchi's *Ugetsu*. Set during a time of war, the film features lovely and quietly fearful images such as a boat lost in thick fog, a mysterious and seductive woman and a ruined country house. *Ugetsu*, based on two stories from Ueda Akinari's book of the same name, is now credited as one of the great films in Japanese cinema and one of the two (along with Akira Kurosawa's

Young sensitive Cole Sear (Haley Joel Osment) imparts dangerous truths to Dr Crowe (Bruce Willis) in *The Sixth Sense* (1999).

*Rashomon*) that introduced many Western viewers to Japanese cinema. In 1964 Masaki Kobayashi's *Kwaidan*, based on several stories from Lafcadio Hearn's collection, also beguiled Western audiences with its combination of the beautiful and the eerie.

A film that was unseen in the West until its release on DVD in 2006 was Nobuo Nakagawa's *Jigoku* (1960). Nakagawa made primarily horror films, and, unlike *Ugetsu* and *Kwaidan*, *Jigoku* is in colour and is surprisingly blood-drenched. It tells the surreal tale of a young man who is increasingly surrounded by death until he, too, dies, and is born into the Japanese Hell of the title. Although *Jigoku* contains its share of memorable images, viewers are more likely to remember the shockingly violent and gruesome torture that its hell-bound ghosts endure.

A Japanese film from 1998 gave the world a new image of the ghost in a plot that played on modern technology. Hideo Nakata's *Ringu* introduced Sadako, the powerful ghost woman whose long black hair perpetually covers her face and hangs down over her featureless white dress. *Ringu*'s ghost curse is passed down by a videotape and telephone, two modern (at the time) technologies that surely would have satisfied M. R. James's requirement that a ghost story be relevant to its audience and not stuck in the past. And yet *Ringu* also echoes traditional Japanese ghost stories by taking the motif of a ghost woman killed in a well from the traditional folktale *Banchō Sarayashiki*. *Ringu* resulted in sequels and a successful American version in 2002, starring Naomi Watts as the reporter investigating the cursed video.

Hong Kong and Korea have also produced notable ghost films. In 1987 Hong Kong's premiere fantasy filmmaker, Tsui Hark, produced *A Chinese Ghost Story*, directed by Ching Siu-tung. If Western audiences had responded to the stately beauty of the early Japanese ghost films, horror fans of the 1980s loved *A Chinese Ghost Story*'s frenetic pace and outrageous images, which included a giant tongue chasing men through a dark forest, a transgendered madam and the manic dance-spells of a Taoist warrior. Based on Pu Songling's *Strange Stories from a Chinese Studio*, the film also involves reincarnation and Chinese history.

Kim Ji-woon of South Korea produced one of the finest ghost films of the decade with *A Tale of Two Sisters* in 2003, which embraced many of the classic tropes of the ghost story – the return to the isolated and gloomy house, the troubled family, the hints of a terrible tragedy in the past, the glimpses of things in shadows. Like *The Sixth Sense*, *A Tale of Two Sisters* climaxes with a revelation about the lead character, in this case a young girl, but it also incorporates elements from other Asian ghost films, such as the ghostly woman with long black hair. Kevin Thomas of the *Los Angeles Times* even compared it to 'Shakespearean tragedy', calling it 'a triumph of stylish, darkly absurdist horror'.[26] It was the first South Korean horror film to receive an American release, and was a hit in its native country.

*La Llorona* has been the subject of several Mexican films, with perhaps the most notable version being *The Curse of the Crying Woman* (1961). The film was produced by and stars Abel Salazar, a key figure in the cycle of Gothic-inspired Mexican horror films produced in the late 1950s and early '60s. This version of *La Llorona* finds her haunting an isolated hacienda, and accompanied by three vicious dogs.

However, the best Spanish-language ghost film ever produced must surely be Guillermo del Toro's *The Devil's Backbone* of 2001. The film is set in a haunted orphanage during the Spanish Civil War, and (as does del Toro's later *Pan's Labyrinth*) features a young child – a boy named Carlos – at the centre of its terror. The film's depiction of its scarred and mutilated ghosts adds a potent element to its social commentary.

An Indian ghost movie from 2003, *Bhoot*, received press because it was a rare Bollywood film that contained no singing or dancing, and took its story of ghostly possession seriously. The film was a box-office smash and scored a Bollywood Movie Award for its director, Ram Gopal Varma.

The first television series to feature a ghostly lead character was *Topper*, based on the same Thorne Smith comic novels that had provided the basis for the film series that began in the 1930s. Cosmo Topper (Leo G. Carroll) is a stuffy businessman who has

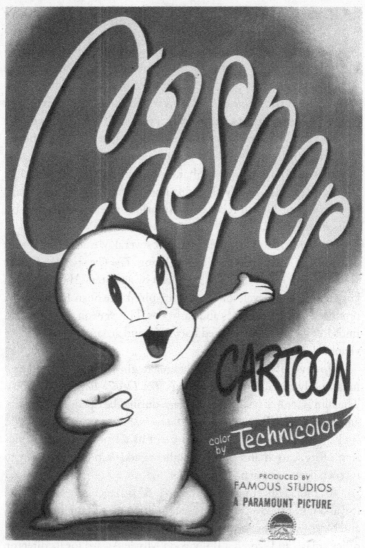

*Casper* cartoon poster, 1950.

recently purchased a house haunted by the fun-loving Kerbys (played by Robert Sterling and Anne Jeffreys). The series, which ran on CBS from 1953 to 1955, is also notable for featuring a ghost dog, the Kerbys' St Bernard, Nell.

In 1959 ABC started running *Casper the Friendly Ghost* cartoons as part of a programme called *Matty's Funday Funnies*. Casper first saw (undead) life in 1945 as a Paramount theatrical cartoon about a cute little boy ghost who, unlike the other ghosts in the haunted house where he lives, would rather befriend humans than frighten them (although he inevitably does a lot of the latter purely by accident). By 1952 Casper was a regular comic-book title from Harvey Comics, and in 1963 ABC gave him his own series. Casper has been before the public non-stop since, and was even the subject of a feature film in 1995.

In the 1950s and '60s most televised horror was presented in anthology shows, with series like *One Step Beyond*, *Boris Karloff's Thriller* and *The Twilight Zone* all offering ghost stories. Perhaps the most famous of these was Rod Serling's adaptation of Lucille Fletcher's radio play 'The Hitch-hiker', which aired during the first season of Serling's *The Twilight Zone*. Playing on the classic urban legend, 'The Hitch-hiker' is also one of the first uses of the twist ending, in which it is revealed that the protagonist is actually the ghost.

Two other series from the 1960s featured ghosts as regular characters: *The Ghost and Mrs Muir* starred Hope Lange and Edward Mulhare in the roles played by Gene Tierney and Rex Harrison in the film of 1947; and the daytime soap opera *Dark Shadows* featured ghosts galore along with vampires, werewolves, witches and assorted other creatures, all contending with one another in the brooding mansion Collinwood. As a daily soap, the series lacked the ability to create complex special effects, but it nevertheless became a cult hit thanks to its spooky plotlines and able cast. The series led to two feature films, *House of Dark Shadows* (1970) and *Night of Dark Shadows* (1971), and in 2012 Tim Burton made a comedic version that centred on the vampiric Barnabas (played by Johnny Depp).

In 1992 the BBC aired a television film that terrified viewers all over Britain and left many believing that they were experiencing paranormal phenomena themselves: *Ghostwatch*. Written by Stephen Volk and directed by Lesley Manning, *Ghostwatch*, which aired on Halloween night, presented its story as a live broadcast of an actual paranormal investigation. It began with a typical poltergeist-style haunting (complete with teenage girl), but soon evolved into a much larger and more frightening paranormal event that eventually spread to the BBC studios in London. The BBC received hundreds of phone calls from viewers who believed the show to be real, and a mentally ill man committed suicide five days after the airing, an act his relatives blamed on the show. The BBC refused to air *Ghostwatch* again, although it has been released on VHS and DVD. Given the response of viewers, *Ghostwatch* must surely be ranked as one of the most realistic ghost films ever made.

Series that featured ghosts as regular characters seemed confined to children's animated programming until the popularity of reality-based series boomed in the 2000s. It was probably only a matter of time before a reality show dedicated to ghost-hunting was made, but even so, its immediate success still came as something of a surprise. *Ghost Hunters* debuted on the Syfy Channel in 2004, and garnered high ratings. It follows two plumbers, Jason Hawes and Grant Wilson, who moonlight as paranormal investigators for TAPS (The Atlantic Paranormal Society). They seek out and visit supposedly haunted sites, spending hours with K-II meters, thermometers, digital voice recorders and digital cameras, gathering measurements and data. The show's presentation employs many of the tropes of a horror film, with jarring music and eerie night-vision shots. The investigators frequently claim that they have been touched or have heard ghostly sounds (often music), and they present everything from small drops in temperature to bursts of static on their audio recordings as 'evidence'. But, despite an onslaught of sceptics who have repeatedly criticized their methods and debunked their findings, the show has generated numerous spin-offs and imitators. There are now dozens of similar shows, with titles like *Scariest Places on Earth*, *Most Haunted*, *Paranormal*

*Challenge* and *Ghost Asylum*. The success of *Ghost Hunters* has also sent the revenue of ghost tourism into the stratosphere.

The popularity of *Ghost Hunters* also generated fictitious television series, most of which – like *Ghost Whisperer* or *Medium* – presented ghosts as tragic figures who needed the help of a good medium to move on. Perhaps the most interesting of recent ghost series was *American Horror Story: Murder House*. The first season of this innovative show – which features a completely different storyline each season, with some recurring cast members – was set in a Victorian house in Los Angeles that attempted to kill and claim the souls of all who lived there. The show's many ghosts were as often pathetic as they were frightening, since they were trapped by the Murder House, forced to endure both their captivity and their fellow ghost captives.

One area of popular culture wherein ghosts have found a surprising home is in videogames. Videogames have come a long way since the days when Pac-Man raced around a dark screen gobbling pellets and trying to avoid ghosts named Blinky, Pinky, Inky and Clyde. In the twenty-first century, one of the hottest game genres is 'survival horror', in which players are thrust into a nightmarish landscape and must try to stay alive while solving some sort of puzzle or mystery. Games like *Silent Hill, Alone in the Dark* and *F.E.A.R.* all involve ghosts that the player must fight or flee from. One of the most unusual of the 'survival horror' games is *Fatal Frame*, in which the player carries not a gun but a camera that can capture ghosts.

Another modern pop-culture invention that offers the chance to experience artificial ghosts in a safe, contained environment is the haunted attraction. Haunted attractions sprang out of the carnival 'dark ride', which typically involved rickety cars on a track rumbling past ghoulish mannequins and stuffed spiders. Walt Disney changed all that in 1969, when he opened the Haunted Mansion attraction in his Disneyland amusement park; the ride incorporated state-of-the-art special effects (some of which, like breathing walls, were plainly inspired by Robert Wise's *The Haunting*) with gorgeous design and a unique transportation system (known as 'Doom

The ghosts of *American Horror Story: Murder House*
are drawn back to the house at dawn (2011).

Buggies') to create the most extravagant dark ride imaginable. The
Haunted Mansion – which features singing sculptures, the disembodied talking head of a medium and an entire ballroom of
whirling, translucent ghosts – inspired legions of future haunters,
and by the 1990s Halloween haunted attractions were starting to
become big business. These haunted houses, once the province of
charity groups and composed of little more than a few rooms with
actors in make-up leaping out at guests, grew increasingly elaborate
and complex. By the 2000s, the haunted attractions industry was
generating an estimated $1 billion in annual revenue, and some very
successful attractions were staying open well past the Halloween
season. Now a haunter – be they professional or amateur – can buy
plasma screens or full-sized animatronic figures (some of which
even talk), providing guests with an experience that is probably far
more exciting than an encounter with a real ghost would be.

Ghosts need not be confined to visual media, however; they
have also proven to be a reliable subject in music. Aside from stan-
dards like Ray Parker Jr's danceable theme song to *Ghostbusters*, or the
much-recorded country classic 'Ghost Riders in the Sky', there are
musical artists who have actually built much of their careers on ghost
music. Before they were in demand in Hollywood, Danny Elfman

(with his band Oingo Boingo) and Rob Zombie were recording such songs as 'Dead Man's Party' and 'Living Dead Girl' respectively. But surely no pop artist has built a career on ghosts in quite the way the British superstar Kate Bush has, beginning in 1978 with 'Wuthering Heights' ('I'm so cold/ Let me in at your window'), extending through playing a ghostly spirit in the video for 'Experiment IV' and culminating in 2014 with the live performance of her avant-garde concept piece 'The Ninth Wave' (1985), in which she appeared as the ghost of a drowned woman haunting her son and husband.

# Conclusion:
# The Ubiquitous Ghost

In the shopping frenzy of Christmas 2014, one item became the season's 'must-buy' gift. It's a board game that has been around for more than 100 years, but sales of it zoomed up over 300 per cent. The item? That hoary hotline to spirits, the Ouija board. Thanks in large part to a critically maligned horror film called *Ouija* (financed in part by Hasbro, the company that produces the Ouija board), it seemed that everyone wanted to get in touch with the Christmas spirit in 2014, despite the warnings of church officials ('It's like opening a shutter in one's soul and letting in the supernatural', said one vicar).[1]

How is it possible that a board game first conceptualized at the height of the nineteenth-century craze for Spiritualism could be a 'must-buy' item in the twenty-first century? And why is a game that consists of no more than a graphically enhanced piece of wood and a plastic planchette still considered 'dangerous' by some?

The answer to the first question is that, quite simply, ghosts are everywhere. They're found in every country, and in every period of history. If the world's entire population could somehow be polled, it is likely that a majority would say they believe in ghosts. A lesser, but still significant, percentage would say that they have had personal experience of a ghost. Many of the world's peoples, both now and in the past, believe that their ancestors are present (at least at certain times of the year), and that an improper burial can create an angry ghost.

A psychologist would suggest that this is how we deal with our feelings of impotent rage when death takes a loved one from us.

Ouija board in action.

We project our emotions outwards, to a safe distance, and create a plate-smashing poltergeist.

Sceptics, meanwhile, counter the true believers at every step. 'It is wonderful', Samuel Johnson noted several hundred years ago, 'that five thousand years have now elapsed since the creation of the world, and still it is undecided whether or not there has ever been an instance of the spirit of any person appearing after death. All argument is against it; but all belief is for it.'[2]

That belief apparently extends to scientists, who seek to discover, measure and even create ghosts (fortunately, their attempts at creating undead spirits have always stopped short of the obvious choice, murder). Amateur scientists venture into the unknown and fumble their way through using gadgets they barely understand; the professionals, meanwhile, manipulate sophisticated technology and theories, but come up with nothing clearer than the tourist holding a K-II meter in a haunted room.

It is obvious that even the most sceptical among us *wants* to believe in ghosts. As we stand in the decaying old mansion, smelling the dust of centuries, feeling the chill of a place that has never known modern heating methods, we can easily imagine the former residents having left something of themselves behind. It doesn't have to be much, certainly not some theatrical special-effects extravaganza of skull-faced creature and blinding light – we do, after all, know better than to believe in *that*. We're willing to accept that as pure fiction; it's the contract we enter into when we open a book or take our seat in the cinema.

But the thought that some part of us might remain behind – even if it's a less than pleasant part, a part motivated by rage or vengeance – holds an undeniable, universal appeal. We are all creatures of ego who find it difficult to imagine that we will, one day, cease; we secretly believe we are too significant for that to happen.

Why, then, are ghosts frightening? Even the Spiritualists, who claimed to find only positive traits in their spirits, were surely touched by that little frisson of fear as they sat in the dark room, listening as the medium's voice roughened. In her classic treatise *On Death and Dying*, Elisabeth Kübler-Ross wrote: 'Death is still a fearful, frightening happening, and the fear of death is a universal fear even if we think we have mastered it on many levels.'[3] Ghosts, as

Ghost graffiti in Tel-Aviv.

Contemporary
Halloween ghost
finger-puppet
toy.

the sort of spiritual trace elements left after death, share in that fearful happening. We are afraid of ghosts because we are afraid of death. Even though they might, on the surface, represent survival after death, we are frustrated because we can't prove it, and frightened because we don't understand it. When we die, will we become a mindless apparition, acting out over and over again some traumatic event? Will we be remembered by our loved ones? Will we be mourned? Will we move on to some other world?

If we fear ghosts, then, why are they so ubiquitous? We see them everywhere these days – in books and cinemas, on television, tattooed on shoulders and spray-painted on urban walls. Perhaps this is our own *Dias de los Muertos*, our way to mock our fears of death. If we make the ghost into a smiling, mischievous ghost-child, we instantly render it down to something we can accept and deal with. Or we can allow it to scare us in the relative safety of a videogame or fake haunted house; we can revel in the adrenaline jolts, and laugh at ourselves later.

One thing is certain: our love of ghosts is not likely to die away any time soon. In the twenty-first century, in the middle of the most advanced civilization the world has ever seen, we still shiver at the thought of a dead friend returning from some otherworld, just as readers of *Gilgamesh* did thousands of years ago. We may fear ghosts, but they unite us and give us a rare common ground. For that reason alone, we should venerate them.

# References

## Introduction

1 Susan Jones, 'Americans' Belief in God Is Strong – But Declining', www.cnsnews.com, 17 December 2013; Leslie Piper, '62 Percent of Americans Would Consider Buying a Haunted Home', *Huffington Post*, 21 October 2013, www.huffingtonpost.com; 'Nearly 87% of Office Workers Believe Ghosts, Gods Real: Poll', *China Post*, 15 August 2011, www.chinapost.com.tw.

## 1 What Are (and Are Not) Ghosts?

1 *The Merriam-Webster New Book of Word Histories* (Springfield, MA, 1991), p. 196.
2 Jonathon Green, *Slang Through the Ages* (Chicago, IL, 1997), p. 332.
3 J. E. Lighter, *Random House Historical Dictionary of American Slang*, vol. 1: *A–G* (New York, 1994), p. 888.
4 T. F. Thiselton Dyer, *The Ghost World* (London, 1898), p. 119.
5 'Gilgamesh, Enkidu and the Nether World: Translation', Electronic Text Corpus of Sumerian Literature (Oxford University), http://etcsl.orinst.ox.ac.uk, accessed February 2015.
6 Herbert Spencer, *The Principles of Sociology* (New York, 1921), vol. 1, p. 829.
7 Rebecca Cathcart, 'Winding Through "Big Dreams" Are the Threads of our Lives', *New York Times*, 3 July 2007, www.nytimes.com.
8 Robert Hunt, *Popular Romances of the West of England; or, the Drolls, Traditions, and Superstitions of Old Cornwall, Second Series* (London, 1865), pp. 156–7.
9 E. T. A. Hoffmann, *The Devil's Elixir* (Edinburgh, 1824), vol. 1, p. 215.
10 Quoted in Daniel Ogden, *Magic, Witchcraft, and Ghosts in the*

*Greek and Roman Worlds: A Sourcebook* (Oxford, 2002), p. 150.

11 Horace Walpole, *The Castle of Otranto* (1764), available at
www.gutenberg.org, accessed February 2015.

12 Lionel A. Weatherly and J. N. Maskelyne, *The Supernatural?*
(London, 1891), p. 110.

13 Sigmund Freud, 'The Uncanny' (1919), available at
www.web.mit.edu, accessed February 2015.


## 2 Lands of the Dead: Early Sightings

1 Theophilus G. Pinches, *The Religion of Babylonia and Assyria*
(London, 1906), p. 107.

2 Donald A. Mackenzie, *Egyptian Myth and Legend* (London,
1909), pp. 177–8.

3 Daniel Ogden, *Magic, Witchcraft, and Ghosts in the Greek and
Roman Worlds: A Sourcebook* (Oxford, 2002), p. 146.

4 Apuleius, *The Works of Apuleius, Comprising the Metamorphoses,
or Golden Ass, The God of Socrates, The Florida, and his Defence,
or a Discourse on Magic* (London, 1866), p. 364.

5 Ovid, *Fasti*, trans. Sir James George Frazer (London, 1959),
Book v, p. 293.

6 Plutarch, *Plutarch's Lives* (London, 1899), vol. v, p. 140.

7 Ovid, *Fasti*, Book II, p. 97.

8 Hesiod, *The Poems and Fragments*, trans. A. W. Mair (Oxford,
1908), p. 60.

9 Virgil, *The Aeneid*, trans. John Dryden, Book II, available at
http://classics.mit.edu, accessed February 2015.

10 Ibid., Book VI.

11 Nicholas Lane, 'Staging Polydorus' Ghost in the Prologue
of Euripides' *Hecuba*', *Classical Quarterly*, LVII/1 (May 2007),
p. 290.

12 Aeschylus, *Four Plays of Aeschylus*, trans. E.D.A. Morshead
(London, 1908), p. 88.

13 *Seneca: Four Tragedies and Octavia*, trans. E. F. Watling
(London, 1970).

14 *Plautus: Three Comedies*, trans. Erich Segal (New York, 1985).

15 N. K. Chadwick, 'Norse Ghosts (A Study in the *Draugr* and
the *Haugbúi*)', *Folklore*, LVII/2 (1943), pp. 54–5.

16 Hermann Pálsson and Paul Edwards, *Eyrbyggja Saga* (New York,
1989), p. 155.

17 Anthony Maxwell, trans., 'The Tale of Thorstein Shiver', in
*The Sagas of Icelanders: A Selection* (New York, 2000), pp. 713–16.

18  Deborah Thompson Prince, 'The "Ghost" of Jesus: Luke 24 in Light of Ancient Narratives of Post-Mortem Apparitions', *Journal for the Study of the New Testament* (March 2007), p. 297.
19  Peter Comestor, *Historia scholastica*, Chapter xxv (Lyon, France, 1539), pp. 104–5.
20  St Thomas, *Summa Theologica*, vol. i, Pt i, p. 572.
21  Quoted in St Augustine, *The Works of Saint Augustine: Letters 156–210: Epistulae II* (New York, 1990), p. 42.
22  Ibid., p. 44.
23  Gregory the Great, *Dialogues*, Book iv (1911), at www.tertullian.org.
24  Ibid.
25  Quoted in David A. Warner, trans., *Ottonian Germany: The Chronicon of Thietmar of Merseburg* (Manchester and New York, 2008), p. 77.
26  Ibid., pp. 75, 77.
27  William of Newburgh, *Historia rerum anglicarum usque ad annum 1198*, quoted in Jean-Claude Schmitt, *Ghosts in the Middle Ages: The Living and the Dead in Medieval Society* (Chicago, il, 1998), p. 62.
28  Dom Augustin Calmet, *Dissertations upon the Apparitions of Angels, Daemons, and Ghosts, and Concerning the Vampires of Hungary, Bohemia, Moravia, and Silesia* (London, 1759), p. 93.
29  John Gmeiner, *The Spirits of Darkness and their Manifestations on Earth: Or, Ancient and Modern Spiritualism* (Milwaukee, wi, 1889), p. 79.
30  Michael Müller, *Triumph of the Blessed Sacrament over the Prince of Evil: History of Nicola Aubry* (1877), quoted in Silent Crusader blog, 10 September 2013, www.catholicsilentcrusade.blogspot.com.
31  The London Hermit, 'A Day with Herne the Hunter', *Dublin University Magazine*, lxxxiv (1874), p. 487.
32  *Chambers's Encyclopædia: A Dictionary of Universal Knowledge* (Philadelphia, pa, 1912), vol. x, p. 656.
33  Lady Wilde, *Ancient Legends, Mystic Charms, and Superstitions of Ireland, with Sketches of the Irish Past* (London, 1902), p. 80.
34  Gladwell Richardson, *Navajo Trader* (Tucson, az, 2003), pp. 99–100.
35  Milwaukee Public Museum, 'Potawatomi Oral Tradition', www.mpm.edu, accessed February 2015.
36  Richard F. Burton, *The Book of the Thousand Nights and a Night* (Denver, co, 1900), vol. iii, p. 252.

37 Joshua Toulmin Smith and Lucy Toulmin Smith, eds, *English Gilds: The Original Ordinances of More than One Hundred Early English Gilds Together with the Olde Usages of the Cite of Wynchestre, the Ordinances of Worcester, the Office of the Mayor of Bristol and the Costomary of the Manor of Tettenhall-Regis* (London, 1870), p. 194.

38 *The Red Dragon: Art of Commanding Spirits* (Pahrump, NV, n.d.), pp. 71–4.

## 3 Rattling Chains and White Sheets: Ghosts in the Western World

1 Baruch Spinoza, 'Letter LVI (LII): Spinoza to Hugo Boxel', www.sacred-texts.com, accessed February 2015.

2 Thomas Hobbes, *Leviathan* (1651), available at www.oregonstate.edu, accessed February 2015.

3 Michael Hunter, 'New Light on the "Drummer of Tedworth": Conflicting Narratives of Witchcraft in Restoration England', *Historical Research*, LXXVIII/201 (2005), pp. 311–53, available at http://eprints.bbk.ac.uk.

4 Samuel Taylor Coleridge, *The Asylum Journal of Mental Science*, April 1858, p. 395.

5 George Cruikshank, *A Discovery Concerning Ghosts: With a Rap at the 'Spirit Rappers'*, 2nd edn (London, 1864), p. 6.

6 Ibid., p. 10.

7 Horace Walpole, *Horace Walpole's Letters* (Philadelphia, PA, 1852), vol. III, p. 169.

8 Charles Ollier, *Fallacy of Ghosts, Dreams, and Omens; With Stories of Witchcraft, Life-in-death, and Monomania* (London, 1848), pp. 21–3.

9 Sarah M. Brownson, *Life of Demetrius Augustine Gallitzin, Prince and Priest* (New York, 1873), p. 101.

10 Francis Xavier Paulhuber, *Bilder des amerikanischen Missions-Lebens in zwölf auserlesenen, in Nord-Amerika gehaltenen Predigten, mit einigen Worten über die Dortigen Erlebnisse* (Freising, Germany, 1864).

11 'Dibbuk (Dybbuk)', *Encyclopedia Judaica* (2008), available at www.jewishvirtuallibrary.org.

12 S. Ansky, trans. S. Morris Engel, *The Dybbuk* (Washington, DC, 1974), p. 123.

13 'The Dibbuk Box', www.dibbukbox.com, accessed February 2015.

14 W.R.S. Ralston, *Russian Folk-tales* (London, 1873), p. 306.

15  Ibid., p. 313.
16  Catherine Crowe, *The Night-side of Nature; or, Ghosts and Ghost Seers* (London, 1848), p. 4.
17  Andrew Jackson Davis, *The Principles of Nature, her Divine Revelations, and a Voice to Mankind*, 32nd edn (Boston, MA, 1871), p. 11.
18  Quoted in Lionel Weatherly and J. N. Maskelyne, *The Supernatural?* (London, 1891), p. 187.
19  Orrin Abbott, *The Davenport Brothers: Their History, Travels, and Manifestations* (New York, 1864), p. 7.
20  Robert Dale Owen, *Footfalls on the Boundary of Another World* (Philadelphia, PA, 1860), p. 212.
21  Abbott, *Davenport Brothers*, p. 40.
22  Newton Crosland, *Apparitions: An Essay* (London, 1873), p. 85.
23  Artemus Ward (Charles F. Browne), *The Complete Works of Artemus Ward* (London, 1898), p. 51.
24  Herbert Spencer, *The Principles of Sociology* (New York, 1906), vol. I, p. 433.
25  John Gmeiner, *The Spirits of Darkness and their Manifestations on Earth: Or, Ancient and Modern Spiritualism* (Milwaukee, WI, 1889), p. 226.
26  Weatherly and Maskelyne, *Supernatural?*, pp. 100–103.
27  *Preliminary Report of the Commission Appointed by the University of Pennsylvania to Investigate Modern Spiritualism in Accordance with the Request of the Late Henry Seybert* (Philadelphia, PA, and London, 1920), p. 159.
28  Carl G. Jung, *Memories, Dreams, Reflections* (New York, 1989), pp. 190–91.
29  Quoted in Charles Chaplin, *My Autobiography* (New York, 1964).
30  Sir Arthur Conan Doyle, *The Wanderings of a Spiritualist* (London, 1921), p. 11.
31  Quoted in Ruth Brandon, *The Life and Many Deaths of Harry Houdini* (New York, 1993), p. 249.
32  Harry Houdini, *A Magician among the Spirits* (New York and London, 1924), p. 172.
33  Mary Roach, *Spook: Science Tackles the Afterlife* (New York, 2005), p. 147.
34  Harry Price, 'The Most Haunted House in England': Ten Years' Investigation of Borley Rectory* (London, 1940), p. 152.
35  Nandor Fodor, *The Haunted Mind: A Psychoanalyst Looks at the Supernatural* (New York, 1968), p. 134.

36 Ibid., p. 171.
37 Quoted in David Bagchi, 'Martin Luther: Ghostbuster', paper given to the Hull & District Theological Society, 25 January 2012, www.hdts.wordpress.com.
38 'Modern Spiritualism', *London Quarterly Review*, CXIV/227 (July 1863), p. 100.
39 Frank Podmore, *The Naturalisation of the Supernatural* (New York and London, 1908), pp. 161–2.
40 Hereward Carrington, *The Story of Psychic Science* (New York, 1931), p. 146.
41 Rupert Matthews, *Haunted London* (Andover, 2012), p. 3.
42 Tom Kington, '"World's Most Haunted Island" Up for Auction', *The Telegraph*, 15 April 2014, www.telegraph.co.uk.
43 'Italy: Shock as Auction for the World's Most Haunted Island is Called Off', *Private Island News*, 26 June 2014, www.privateislandnews.com.
44 Laura Vecsey, 'New Orleans' LaLaurie House Has Gruesome Past', www.forbes.com, 23 October 2013.
45 'The Original Ghost Walk of York', www.theoriginalghostwalkofyork.co.uk, accessed February 2015.
46 Jay Anson, *The Amityville Horror* (New York, 1977), pp. 288–9.
47 Joe Nickell, 'Amityville: The Horror of It All', *Skeptical Inquirer*, XXVII/1 (January/February 2003).
48 Matt Soniak, 'Elva Zona Heaster: The Ghost who Helped Solve her Own Murder', *Mental Floss*, 24 September 2014, www.mentalfloss.com.
49 John O'Brien, 'Back from the Grave? Did Teresita Basa Enter Another Person's Body and Name her Murderer? The Police Have No Other Explanation', *St Petersburg Independent*, 6 March 1978.
50 'Murder Convict Wins Retrial because Jury Members Used Ouija Board', *AP News Archive*, 25 October 1994, www.apnewsarchive.com.
51 'Many Americans Mix Multiple Faiths', *Pew Research Center*, 9 December 2009, www.pewforum.org.

## 4 Hungry Ghosts: The Eastern World

1 Francis Hsu, *Under the Ancestors' Shadow: Chinese Culture and Personality* (New York, 1948), p. 144.
2 Arthur Waley, *The Nine Songs: A Study of Shamanism in Ancient China* (London, 1955), p. 11.

3 Ban Gu, *Hanshu*, quoted in Luo Hui, *The Ghost of Liaozhai: Pu Songling's Ghostlore and its History of Reception* (Toronto, ON, 2009), p. 39.

4 Jan J. M. de Groot, 'Buddhist Masses for the Dead at Amoy', *Actes du sixième congrès international des orientalistes* (Leiden, Netherlands, 1885), Pt 4, Sect. 4, pp. 20–21.

5 Stephen F. Tessier, *The Ghost Festival in Medieval China* (Princeton, NJ, 1988), pp. 127–9.

6 'The Hungry Ghost Festival', www.discoverhongkong.com, accessed February 2015.

7 Leo Tak-hung Chan, *The Discourse on Foxes and Ghosts: Ji Yun and Eighteenth-century Literati Storytelling* (Honolulu, HI, 1998), p. 26.

8 Pu Songling, *Strange Stories from a Chinese Studio* (New York, 1925), p. 62.

9 'Top 8 Haunted Places in Beijing', *China Daily*, 8 August 2014, www.chinadaily.com.cn.

10 Michelle Yun, 'Ghosts Create Bargains in Hong Kong Housing', *Bloomberg Business*, 20 November 2014, www.bloomberg.com.

11 Tiffany Lam, 'Haunted Hong Kong: Read if You Dare', *CNN*, 25 October 2011, www.travel.cnn.com.

12 Michiko Iwasaka and Barre Toelken, *Ghosts and the Japanese: Cultural Experience in Japanese Death Legends* (Logan, UT, 1994), p. 6.

13 Lafcadio Hearn, *Kwaidan: Stories and Studies of Strange Things* (Leipzig, Germany, 1907), pp. 15–16.

14 Brent Swancer, 'The Mysterious Suicide Forest of Japan', *Mysterious Universe*, 9 May 2014, www.mysteriousuniverse.org.

15 W. Y. Evans-Wentz, *The Tibetan Book of the Dead* (Oxford, 1960), pp. 164–5.

16 William Crooke, *The Popular Religion and Folk-lore of Northern India* (Westminster, 1896), vol. I, p. 153.

17 Ibid., p. 246.

18 Ruth S. Freed and Stanley A. Freed, *Ghosts: Life and Death in North India* (Seattle, WA, 1993), p. 15.

19 Ibid., p. 176.

20 Sir George Grey, *Polynesian Mythology, and Ancient Traditional History of the New Zealand Race, as Furnished by their Priests and Chiefs* (London, 1855), p. 18.

## 5 *La Llorona* and Dreamtime: Ghosts in Latin America and the Southern Hemisphere

1 F. Gonzalez-Crussi, *The Day of the Dead and Other Mortal Reflections* (San Diego, CA, 1974), p. 71.
2 Lynn Meisch, *A Traveler's Guide to El Dorado and the Inca Empire* (New York, 1977), p. 399.
3 Alfred Avila, *Mexican Ghost Tales of the Southwest* (Houston, TX, 1994), p. 106.
4 Patrick Tierney, *The Highest Altar: The Story of Human Sacrifice* (London, 1989), pp. 33–4.
5 Harold Osborne, *South American Mythology* (Middlesex, 1968), pp. 119–22.
6 Daniel Biebuyck and Kahombo C. Mateene, *The Mwindo Epic from the Banyanga (Zaire)* (Berkeley and Los Angeles, CA, 1969), p. 5.
7 A. B. Ellis, *The Yoruba-speaking Peoples of the Slave Coast of West Africa* (London, 1894), p. 137.
8 Ibid., p. 139.
9 Amos Tutuola, *The Village Witch Doctor and Other Stories* (London, 1990), pp. 1–11.
10 Nathaniel Samuel Murrell, *Afro-Caribbean Religions: An Introduction to their Historical, Cultural, and Sacred Traditions* (Philadelphia, PA, 2010), p. 261.
11 James Dawson, *Australian Aborigines: The Languages and Customs of Several Tribes of Aborigines in the Western District of Victoria, Australia* (Melbourne, 1881), pp. 50–51.
12 Patrick McNamara, *Spirit Possession and Exorcism: History, Psychology, and Neurobiology*, vol. I, *Mental States and the Phenomenon of Possession* (Santa Barbara, CA, 2011), p. 159.
13 Stefanie Anderson, 'The 18 Most Haunted Places in Australia that You Can Actually Visit', www.buzzfeed.com, 30 October 2014.

## 6 The Quest for Evidence: The Ghost and Science

1 Aaron Sagers, 'Paranormal Community Reacts to Death of Ghostbuster Harold Ramis', *HuffPost Weird News*, 26 February 2014, www.huffingtonpost.com.
2 Tom Cook, quoted in Benjamin Radford, 'The Shady Science of Ghost Hunting', www.livescience.com, 27 October 2006.
3 Newton Crosland, *Apparitions: An Essay* (London, 1873), p. 32.

4 Quoted in B. C. Forbes, 'Edison Working on How to
  Communicate with the Next World', *American Magazine*, XC
  (October 1920), p. 10.
5 Kenny Biddle, 'Testing the K-II EMF Meter: Does It Communicate
  with Spirits? No', James Randi Educational Foundation,
  24 September 2014, http://web.randi.org.
6 See, for example, www.ubu.com/sound/occult.html.
7 'LaserGrid GS1', www.ghoststop.com, accessed February 2015.
8 Steve Gonsalves, 'Using the Thermal Imaging Camera',
  www.syfy.com, accessed February 2015.
9 Troy Taylor, 'Spirit Photography: Its Strange and Controversial
  History', The Haunted Museum, www.prairieghosts.com, accessed
  February 2015.
10 P. T. Barnum, *Humbugs of the World: An Account of Humbugs,
  Delusions, Impositions, Quackeries, Deceits, and Deceivers Generally,
  in All Ages* (New York, 1866), p. 119.
11 Andy Dolan, 'Mystery of Wem Ghost Solved by an 88-year-old
  Postcard and an Eagle-eyed Pensioner', *Daily Mail*, 19 May 2010,
  www.dailymail.co.uk.
12 '21 Heavenly Spirit Orbs Photos', www.beliefnet.com, accessed
  February 2015.
13 'Ghost Hangs around Disneyland', www.youtube.com, accessed
  February 2015.
14 Nandor Fodor, 'The Poltergeist – Psychoanalyzed', *Psychiatric
  Quarterly*, April 1948, reprinted in Hereward Carrington,
  *Haunted People* (New York, 1968), p. 182.
15 Rense Lange and James Houran, 'Induced Paranormal Experiences:
  Support for Houran and Lange's Model of Haunting Phenomena',
  *Perceptual and Motor Skills*, LXXXIV (June 1997), p. 1455.
16 Richard Wiseman, 'The Haunted Brain', *Skeptical Inquirer*,
  XXXV/5 (September/October 2011).
17 R. Bunton-Stasyshyn and R. Davis, 'The "Haunt" Project: An
  Attempt to Build a "Haunted" Room by Manipulating Complex
  Electromagnetic Fields and Infrasound', *Cortex*, XLV/5 (May 2009),
  pp. 619–29.
18 Wiseman, 'The Haunted Brain'.
19 Vic Tandy and Tony R. Lawrence, 'The Ghost in the Machine',
  *Journal of the Society for Psychical Research*, LXII/851 (April 1998).
20 Michelle Roberts, 'Chopin "Probably Had Epilepsy"', BBC News:
  Health, 25 January 2011, www.bbc.co.uk.

## 7 From King Richard to *Paranormal Activity*: The Ghost in Literature, Film and Popular Culture

1 S. T. Joshi, *The Weird Tale* (Holicong, PA, 2003), p. 142.
2 M. R. James, 'From the Preface to *More Ghost Stories of an Antiquary* (1911)', in *Collected Ghost Stories* (Oxford, 2011), pp. 406–7.
3 Julia Briggs, *Night Visitors: The Rise and Fall of the English Ghost Story*, quoted in Joshi, *The Weird Tale*, p. 2.
4 Horace Walpole, *The Castle of Otranto* (1764), available at www.gutenberg.org, accessed February 2015.
5 Ann Radcliffe, *The Mysteries of Udolpho* (1794), available at www.gutenberg.org, accessed February 2015.
6 Walter Scott, 'The Tapestried Chamber; or, The Lady in the Sacque' (1831), available at www.gutenberg.org, accessed February 2015.
7 Ibid.
8 J. Sheridan Le Fanu, 'An Account of Some Strange Disturbances in Aungier Street' (1853), available at http://gaslight.mtroyal.ca/aungier.htm, accessed February 2015.
9 Ibid.
10 Charles Dickens, *A Christmas Carol* (1843), available at www.gutenberg.org, accessed February 2015.
11 Henry James, *The Turn of the Screw* (1898), available at www.gutenberg.org, accessed February 2015.
12 Shirley Jackson, *The Haunting of Hill House* (New York, 1959), p. 1.
13 Quoted in John J. Miller, 'Chilling Fiction', *Wall Street Journal*, 29 October 2009, www.wsj.com.
14 Ibid.
15 Matthew R. Bradley, 'Richard Matheson – Storyteller: Fresh Hell', www.tor.com, 9 November 2010.
16 Stephen King, *The Shining* (Garden City, NY, 1977), p. 216.
17 Peter Straub, *Ghost Story* (New York, 1979), p. 414.
18 Peter Valenti, 'The "Film *Blanc*": Suggestions for a Variety of Fantasy, 1940–45', *Journal of Popular Film*, VI/4 (1978), pp. 294–304.
19 'Scorsese's Scariest Movies of All Time', *Daily Beast*, 31 October 2014, www.thedailybeast.com.
20 Vincent Canby, '"Ghost Story" Tells of 50-year-old Mystery', *New York Times*, 16 December 1981, www.nytimes.com.
21 'Scorsese's Scariest Movies of All Time'.
22 Roger Ebert, '*The Shining*', 18 June 2006, www.rogerebert.com.
23 *Variety* Staff, 'Review: *The Shining*', *Variety*, 31 December 1979, www.variety.com.

24 Quoted in Joe Dunthorne, 'Was Stephen King Right to Hate Stanley Kubrick's *Shining?*', *The Guardian*, 6 April 2013, www.theguardian.com.
25 Ben Child, 'Here's Johnny! The Shining Scene is Scariest in Movie History, Claims Study', *The Guardian*, 31 October 2013, www.theguardian.com.
26 Kevin Thomas, 'A Stylish and Creepy Korean "Tale"', *Los Angeles Times*, 17 December 2004, http://articles.latimes.com.

## Conclusion: The Ubiquitous Ghost

1 Neil Tweedie, 'Sales of Ouija Boards up 300% and Threatening to Become a Christmas "Must Buy" Despite Warning from Churchmen', *Daily Mail*, 30 November 2014, www.dailymail.co.uk.
2 James Boswell, *The Life of Samuel Johnson, LLD* (London, 1846), vol. VII, p. 59.
3 Elisabeth Kübler-Ross, *On Death and Dying* (New York, 1970), p. 5.

# Select Bibliography

Anson, Jay, *The Amityville Horror* (New York, 1977)

Avila, Alfred, *Mexican Ghost Tales of the Southwest* (Houston, TX, 1994)

Calmet, Dom Augustin, *Dissertations upon the Apparitions of Angels, Daemons, and Ghosts, and Concerning the Vampires of Hungary, Bohemia, Moravia, and Silesia* (London, 1759)

Carrington, Hereward, *The Story of Psychic Science* (New York, 1931)

Clarke, Roger, *A Natural History of Ghosts: 500 Years of Hunting for Proof* (London, 2012)

Crooke, William, *The Popular Religion and Folk-lore of Northern India*, vol. I (Westminster, 1896)

Crosland, Newton, *Apparitions: An Essay* (London, 1873)

Crowe, Catherine, *The Night-side of Nature; or, Ghosts and Ghost Seers* (London, 1848)

Cruikshank, George, *A Discovery Concerning Ghosts: With a Rap at the 'Spirit Rappers'*, 2nd edn (London, 1864)

Davies, Owen, *The Haunted: A Social History of Ghosts* (London, 2009)

Dawson, James, *Australian Aborigines: The Languages and Customs of Several Tribes of Aborigines in the Western District of Victoria, Australia* (Melbourne, 1881)

Ellis, A. B., *The Yoruba-speaking Peoples of the Slave Coast of West Africa* (London, 1894)

Evans-Wentz, W. Y., *The Tibetan Book of the Dead* (Oxford, 1960)

Finucane, R. C., *Ghosts: Appearances of the Dead and Cultural Transformation* (Amherst, MA, 2002)

Fodor, Nandor, *Haunted People* (New York, 1968)

Freed, Ruth S., and Stanley A. Freed, *Ghosts: Life and Death in North India* (Seattle, WA, 1993)

Gmeiner, John, *The Spirits of Darkness and their Manifestations on Earth: Or, Ancient and Modern Spiritualism* (Milwaukee, WI, 1889)

Hearn, Lafcadio, *Kwaidan: Stories and Studies of Strange Things* (Leipzig, Germany, 1907)

Iwasaka, Michiko, and Barre Toelken, *Ghosts and the Japanese: Cultural Experience in Japanese Death Legends* (Logan, UT, 1994)

Joshi, S. T., *The Weird Tale* (Holicong, PA, 2003)

Mackenzie, Donald A., *Egyptian Myth and Legend* (London, 1909)

Maxwell, Anthony, trans., 'The Tale of Thorstein Shiver', in *The Sagas of Icelanders: A Selection* (New York, 2000)

Morton, Lisa, *The Halloween Encyclopedia*, 2nd edn (Jefferson City, MO, 2011)

Murrell, Nathaniel Samuel, *Afro-Caribbean Religions: An Introduction to their Historical, Cultural, and Sacred Traditions* (Philadelphia, PA, 2010)

Ogden, Daniel, *Magic, Witchcraft, and Ghosts in the Greek and Roman Worlds: A Sourcebook* (Oxford, 2002)

Ollier, Charles, *Fallacy of Ghosts, Dreams, and Omens; With Stories of Witchcraft, Life-in-death, and Monomania* (London, 1848)

Ovid, *Fasti*, trans. Sir James George Frazer (London, 1959), Book V

Owen, Robert Dale, *Footfalls on the Boundary of Another World* (Philadelphia, PA, 1860)

Pálsson, Hermann, and Paul Edwards, *Eyrbyggja Saga* (New York, 1989)

Price, Harry, *'The Most Haunted House in England': Ten Years' Investigation of Borley Rectory* (London, 1940)

Pu Songling, *Strange Stories from a Chinese Studio* (New York, 1925)

Roach, Mary, *Spook: Science Tackles the Afterlife* (New York, 2005)

Schmitt, Jean-Claude, *Ghosts in the Middle Ages: The Living and the Dead in Medieval Society* (Chicago, IL, 1998)

Tessier, Stephen F., *The Ghost Festival in Medieval China* (Princeton, NJ, 1988)

Thiselton Dyer, T. F., *The Ghost World* (London, 1898)

Tutuola, Amos, *The Village Witch Doctor and Other Stories* (London, 1990)

Weatherly, Lionel A., and J. N. Maskelyne, *The Supernatural?* (London, 1891)

Wicker, Christine, *Lily Dale: The True Story of the Town that Talks to the Dead* (New York, 2003)

# Acknowledgements &
# Photo Acknowledgements

Thank you to my agent, Robert Fleck; to Dan Weinstein and the entire staff of the Iliad Bookshop; to Rocky Wood, who provided both material and enthusiasm; to Stephen Jones, who gave me amazing insight into haunted London; my partner, Ricky Grove, and my family; to the entire crew at Reaktion Books; and especially to my extraordinarily patient editor, Ben Hayes, whose support deserves more than the silly ghost joke I was going to make here.

# Index